OXFORDSHIRE
UNCORKED

A GUIDE TO THE VINEYARDS AND WINES
OF OXFORDSHIRE AND NORTH COTSWOLDS

©2024 Marcus Rees &
Meze Publishing Limited
First edition printed in 2024 in the UK
ISBN: 978-1-915538-24-6
Written by: Marcus Rees
Edited by: Emily Readman, Holly Dibden
Photography by: Paul Gregory
Additional Photos P70-77: Ed Dallimore
Designed by: Paul Cocker
Sales & Marketing: Emma Toogood
Printed and bound in the UK by
Bell & Bain Ltd, Glasgow

Published by Meze Publishing Limited
Unit 1b, 2 Kelham Square
Kelham Riverside
Sheffield S3 8SD
Web: www.mezepublishing.co.uk
Telephone: 0114 275 7709
Email: info@mezepublishing.co.uk

FOREWORD
IAN BEECHER-JONES, CHAIR OF THAMES AND CHILTERNS VINEYARDS ASSOCIATION

Congratulations to Marcus and the team for compiling this wonderful guide that showcases the vineyards of Oxfordshire and the North Cotswolds.

The Thames and Chilterns region is an unsung hotspot for English vineyards. The chalk hills of the Chilterns and the gravel sands of the Thames Valley allow for a wonderful and distinctive style of wine.

The fabulous vineyards in the region are relatively new compared to other parts of the country, but they offer a vibrant and unique addition to England's wine industry.

As Chair of the Thames and Chilterns Vineyards Association, I'm proud to be a grower in this wonderful region, and we look forward to welcoming you to our vineyards to enjoy our wines.

Ian Beecher-Jones

WINEGB
THAMES & CHILTERNS

CONTENTS

INTRODUCTION

The world of English wine is an exciting and fast-changing place. I have a rather good, though now outdated, guide to the wines of England and Wales written in 2008 by Phillip Williamson, David Moore and Neville Blech. It lists just four vineyards in Oxfordshire - two of which no longer exist. Fast forward 16 years to 2024, and there are now 14 commercial vineyards selling wine.

Wine GB (www.winegb.co.uk) has a wealth of interesting statistics on the industry's growth. For example, its 2023 Industry Report shows the enormous growth in recent years in both production and total area planted with vines, with the latter increasing by 74% in the last five years alone. Projected growth shows no sign of abating, with 600 hectares of vines already planted but not yet in active production. The record production of around 21 million bottles in 2023, helped by a bumper harvest following a wet summer with a warm spell at the end, delivered a staggering 60% increase on the previous record of 13.1 million bottles in the hot, sunny year of 2018.

In such a fast-moving environment, it is difficult to keep track of the plethora of joys available on our doorstep, and that is why I wrote this book. Even useful websites, such as the Thames and Chilterns Vineyards Association, or apps such as Cellar Door, are limited in one way or another. First and foremost, I wanted this guide to be practical and useful and to encourage readers to try the wines and visit the producers. Many of the featured venues, as well as offering tours and tastings, regularly host additional events such as jazz evenings, wine-blending workshops, and even weddings. There are so many enjoyable ways to experience Oxfordshire and the surrounding region's wine scene.

As I met the owners and producers featured in this book, I discovered several recurring themes. Firstly, nearly all the featured vineyards and wineries are small, artisanal family operations, run by individuals or couples with a great passion for making quality produce. It's a very different scale to some of the larger producers in Kent and Sussex, now with hundreds of hectares and up to a million bottles per year (themselves dwarfed by the bigger Champagne houses producing 10 to 20 million bottles per year). Secondly, it was repeatedly remarked that many people remained unaware of their local wine producers, even when situated just a few miles up the road. I hope this book encourages readers to visit their local vineyards and to try their wines. If you do, then it will have succeeded in one of its main objectives: to help grow the local visitor economy in Oxfordshire. I am grateful to OxLep (Oxfordshire Local Enterprise Partnership) for recognising the potential of this book and for helping make its publication possible.

One common question that the producers are frequently asked is: "Why is English wine so expensive?" The answer is complicated, but one of the main reasons why English wines are more expensive than countries such as France, Italy, New Zealand and South Africa, is because the yields are so much smaller - the same area of land and the same amount of work produces a great deal less wine. Also, small producers do not benefit from the economies of scale that large producers enjoy. Another answer to that question is that English wine isn't expensive at all. Our world-class sparkling wines, making up 70% of England's total wine production, are every bit as good value as any other traditional method sparkling wine you might find on a supermarket shelf. And £10 to £20 for a bottle of still wine – one that has been carefully crafted by dedicated local producers, and enjoyed, perhaps, on-site within view of the vines, or during a tour with the winemaker – strikes me as extremely good value. Time and again, I was struck by how delicious the still wines produced here are, both white and red, and it makes me excited for the future.

In order to make this guide as comprehensive as possible, I have also included five vineyards in the neighbouring counties of Berkshire, Buckinghamshire, and Gloucestershire. This was in recognition of their proximity, as well as the fact that many of Oxfordshire's visitors also venture to the Cotswolds, and therefore might enjoy a visit to Little Oak or Poulton Hill. The three featured vineyards in Berkshire and Buckinghamshire all have wineries on-site, and two of them have direct links to some of Oxfordshire's vineyards as producers of their wines. There are, of course, other excellent vineyards in all three counties, and I hope you enjoy exploring them once you have exhausted this book.

I wanted to feature all the 'commercial' vineyards in Oxfordshire, by which I mean their wines are commercially available to the public. As not all of them could be featured, the vineyards that were unable to participate are listed at the back of the book. In addition, there are several Oxfordshire vineyards outside the scope of this book. Yew Tree Vineyard in West Hagbourne is run by Ed Mitcham, and he helps manage several of the vineyards featured here. The fruit is sold to urban wineries who use the grapes to make their own wines. There are also several small, amateur vineyards run predominantly as hobbies or for non-commercial production. These include Dreaming Squires, close to Raymond Blanc's Le Manoir aux Quat' Saisons in Great Milton. They produce astonishingly good still white wines for an amateur set-up.

I hope this book encourages you to visit some places you didn't know about, to enjoy their hospitality and their produce, and continue your support of the amazing wineries and vineyards that England has to offer.

ABOUT ME

I fell in love with Oxfordshire in 1990 when I was lucky enough to attend university in Oxford. Back then, Mic Young, the superb runner of Lincoln College's bar, used to organise trips to the Oxfordshire countryside to visit real ale pubs, and it was on these trips that I was struck by the beauty of places such as Finstock, Great Milton and Long Wittenham. After I left university I lived in Dorking, Surrey for seven years, right opposite Denbies Vineyard, which is one of England's largest. I always remember having a burning desire to stay at their on-site B&B despite living only 200 yards away.

For around 20 years, I used to make annual visits to France with my brother and a friend. We'd cycle around the different wine regions, then fill up the car with as much wine as we could from the producers we had met along the way. One year, all of us pressed for time, we decided to have a short weekend near Hastings instead, cycling around a handful of small producers in Kent and Sussex. We were amazed by the quality of the wines we tasted, and it was on that trip that I first realised just how good English wine could be, as well as how many vineyards were springing up around the country.

After a few years in Buckinghamshire, I moved back to Oxfordshire in 2010 and have since lived in Witney, Minster Lovell, Charlbury and Wallingford. Wherever I've lived, I've loved exploring the beautiful Cotswold and Chiltern Hills on my bicycle, and it has always motivated me to know that I can find a good pint of ale en route at a pub or a brewery. But increasingly, a chilled glass of wine at a local winery or vineyard has become an option too, and what an enjoyable one it is.

When not writing or cycling, I spend a lot of time guiding tourists around Oxfordshire and the Cotswolds. Local vineyards are featuring more and more on my tours, and I hope to see you at one soon.

Marcus Rees

THE WINERIES
& VINEYARDS

BRIDEWELL GARDENS

Contact Details:
The Walled Garden,
Wilcote,
North Leigh,
Oxfordshire,
OX7 3DT
01993 259 059

What3Words:
//scarves.rivers.initiated

Website & Socials:
www.bridewellgardens.org
@bridewellgardens
info@bridewellgardens.org

Visitor Centre:
No, but Bridewell hosts open days throughout the year.

Tours:
None available.

Established: 1997

First Vintage Released: 2004

Size: 2 hectares

Grapes Grown:
Orion, Phoenix, Regent

Annual Production:
c 1,500 bottles

First and foremost, Bridewell is a mental health recovery charity that provides support through therapeutic horticulture. Set up in 1994 within a derelict walled garden, the area where the vineyard is located was later leased in 1997 and planted in 2000. Since then, Bridewell have developed all areas of the garden and vineyard, and both are maintained by service users as part of their recovery. Recovering adults are of all ages and from all walks of life.

BRIDEWELL GARDENS

Bridewell has just nine paid staff (mainly part-time), around 30 volunteers and 40-90 service users at any one time. Service users typically spend two days a week at Bridewell over a six-month to two-year period. Morning activities might include composting or weeding in the walled garden, while afternoons are typically spent pruning, bud-rubbing, and stripping the vines. During quieter times of the year, service users are kept busy collecting eggs from the resident chickens, as well as being encouraged to take part in decision-making and the development of the organisation. Working at the vineyard can be very beneficial for someone recovering from poor mental health: it provides an opportunity to work closely with others in a compassionate and supportive environment, with the additional benefit that, once the wines have been made, service users can, quite literally, see the fruits of their labour.

The vineyard sits on a south-facing slope and escapes most of the local frosts. It is certified organic, which was one of Bridewell's objectives from the beginning. Orion and Phoenix varieties were selected with this in mind, and all the planting has been done by hand. Bridewell has a very informal approach to their training, leaning more upon a great deal of passion and some local horticultural advice. The vineyard has never been sprayed and yet has never suffered an attack from dreaded mildew, and any weeds are kept in close check so they don't suffocate the vines. The vineyard boundaries are planted with thyme, olive trees, lavender, and rosemary bushes to provide biodiversity, and the sheltering birch trees and poplars are routinely thinned to reduce the amount of shade cast on the vines.

Bridewell's sparkling wine is a roughly equal blend of Orion and Phoenix, but this varies from year to year depending on the harvest. Time is never considered wasted when the harvest is less fruitful, as the vines' primary role of aiding recovery far outweighs their financial benefits. Bridewell's vineyard model has been so successful that other crops, for example flowers, might be developed on-site in the future.

Bridewell's wines, including the 2018 and 2019 vintages, have long been made at Davenport, based in Sussex and Kent. The 2020 and 2021 pandemic harvests were sold as fruit; 2022's vintage was made locally in Oxfordshire; and the 2023 vintage, not yet for sale, will see a new collaboration with the English Wine Project in Derbyshire. All Bridewell's wines are certified organic and made using the traditional method.

Unsurprisingly, their production sells out each year, so not many stockists are needed. Eynsham Cellars, however, is a long-standing local partner and stockist. Others include Charbury Deli, Café de la Poste in Chadlington, and the Teardrop Bar in Oxford's Covered Market.

Wilcote Brut

Vintage: 2019   **ABV:** 11%

Grapes: Orion, Phoenix

Typical Retail Price: £25

Nose: Baked apple and pear drops.

Palate: A very fine mousse, pleasant balance of fruit and acidity, and good length.

Comments: A refreshing, organic English fizz; 2019 was the last vintage made at Davenport.

"Bridewell made me feel supported, believed, encouraged, boosted, able to be myself. It made me feel safe & understood, fortunate & joyful."

Bridewell Organic Gardens

WILCOTE

2019

Quality Sparkling Wine

Brut   Orion/Phoenix

Produced for Bridewell Organic Gardens by Davenport Vineyards,
Limney Farm, Castle Hill, Rotherfield, E Sussex, TN6 3RR UK

75cle   11% vol

BRIGHTWELL VINEYARD

Contact Details:
Rush Court, Shillingford Road,
Wallingford OX10 8LJ
01491 832 354

What3Words:
///radiated.sweetened.goal

Website & Socials:
www.brightwellvineyard.co.uk
@brightwell.vineyard
info@brightwellvineyard.co.uk

Visitor Centre: The vineyard shop is usually open year-round, Friday-Sunday, 12-6pm. At other times, wine can be purchased from the vineyard house. Events include the Thames Valley Food & Drink Festival, which takes place in June.

Tours: One and two-hour tours, around £20pp, including three to five tasting wines. These are every weekend, from June to September, and must be pre-booked. Private tours of 10 people or above can be arranged by appointment year-round. They also have a hireable event space by the lakeside, near the River Thames, that's available June to September.

Established: 1987

Current Owners' First Vintage Released: 2001

Size: 6 hectares

Grapes Grown: Bacchus, Chardonnay, Huxelrebe, Dornfelder, Pinot Noir, Reichensteiner

Annual Production: 20,000-30,000 bottles

Brightwell Vineyard is situated on the River Thames, about one and a half miles north of Wallingford. It was first planted in the late 1980s and was taken over by the current owners, Bob and Carol Nielsen, in 1999. Their first vintages, from 2001, were made at nearby Stanlake Park in Berkshire and proved promising, but Bob, who now manages the winemaking, was eager to take control and satisfy his desire to experiment and improve; to him, the role of winemaker is like that of a chef.

FRANCOIS FRERES
TONNELLERIE
ST ROMAIN CÔTE D'OR
FRANCE
GF
M
20
PINOT
2011

BRIGHTWELL VINEYARD

Presses, tanks and other equipment were gradually acquired, mainly second-hand, from Suffolk, Herefordshire, Kent and France. In 2011, the first Brightwell wines to be made entirely on-site were produced. An Australian winemaker was employed initially, but now self-taught Bob takes the lead, driven by his desire to see how good English wine can be. From the start, Brightwell focused its range on still wines, reasoning that the market for still wines is much bigger than sparkling wines. Brightwell's production expanded again in 2014.

Bob and Carol planted all Pinot Noir in the vineyard, and Bob is particularly fond of making red wines because of the additional variables they offer. He says, "You can experiment more with reds", and revels in the challenge of excelling in an area where few English producers focus their efforts. Bob believes that the more difficult the vines are to grow, the better the wines are that they produce, and it's this dedication that makes Brightwell's red wines so delicious.

Their grape varieties, yeasts and blends have all changed over the years and will continue to do so. The Reichensteiner is not currently bottled and sold as a wine, but it's used in Brightwell's Rush English brandy, which is aged in oak casks and available online and at the vineyard. Bob and Carol's most recent planting of Sauvignon Blanc is set to expand their range in future.

Carol takes care of sales while Bob manages production. The family also help out, and local volunteers are recruited for the October harvest, alongside paid workers. Bob considers his production process – which maximises resources and efficiency – to be intrinsically sustainable; this includes collecting rainwater, composting grape skins, and even reusing disposable cups.

Stockists include the Oxford Wine Company, with outlets in Oxford, Standlake and Millets Farm; several local Waitrose supermarkets, including Wallingford; the Cookhouse Deli in Wallingford; and other independent farm shops.

BRIGHTWELL VINEYARD

Food

COMPLAINT DEPT.

PLEASE
TAKE A NUMBER

A few facts and figures about
English & Welsh wines and vineyards
2017

Number of
commercial vineyards:
502

Annual production

Oxford Flint

Vintage: 2019   **ABV:** 12%

Grapes: Huxelrebe

Typical Retail Price: £13

Nose: Light, zesty citrus.

Palate: Clean and subtle with appealing acidity.

Comments: Reminiscent of Muscadet, this wine is unoaked and makes a great aperitif.

Oxford Gold

Vintage: 2017   **ABV:** 13%

Grapes: Huxelrebe

Typical Retail Price: £13

Nose: Tropical fruit including mango.

Palate: Tropical fruit and spice, with good structure and mouthfeel.

Comments: An off-dry wine with any residual sugar being nicely balanced by its acidity; reminiscent of some Alsace wines.

Oxford Rosé

Vintage: 2021   **ABV:** 12%

Grapes: Dornfelder

Typical Retail Price: £12

Nose: Savoury and floral.

Palate: Dry and savoury with a hint of strawberry fruit.

Comments: A refreshing and dry style of rosé.

Sparkling Chardonnay

Vintage: 2010   **ABV:** 11%

Grapes: Chardonnay

Typical Retail Price: £25

Nose: Subtle with lime zest, petals, and a hint of bread and butter pudding.

Palate: Strawberry and citrus fruit with a very fine fizz.

Comments: Aged on the lees for three years; tastes surprisingly fresh and zesty despite its age.

Oxford Regatta

Vintage: 2018   **ABV:** 12%

Grapes: Dornfelder

Typical Retail Price: £14

Nose: Tobacco, leather and blackberries.

Palate: Damson and berry fruit; a light body and plenty of acidity lead into a long finish.

Comments: 2018 was a long, hot summer and this is a lovely red wine, aged in oak barrels to soften the tannins.

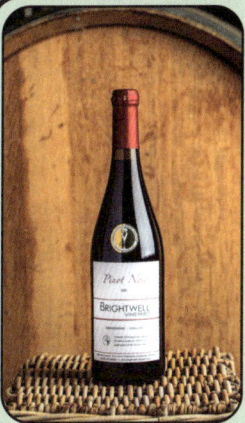

Pinot Noir

Vintage: 2018   **ABV:** 12%

Grapes: Pinot Noir

Typical Retail Price: £16

Nose: Cedar, leather, herbs and spices.

Palate: Savoury, structured and balanced, with a light body and light oak character.

Comments: A complex and delicious wine which demonstrates why English wine is so exciting.

CHILTERN VALLEY WINERY AND BREWERY

Contact Details:
Old Luxters Vineyard,
Hambleden, Henley-on-Thames,
Oxfordshire, RG9 6JW
01491 638 330

What3Words:
///steam.afternoon.putts

Website & Socials:
www.chilternvalley.co.uk
@chilternvalleywinerybrewery
enquiries@chilternvalley.co.uk

Visitor Centre: Yes, comprising a well-stocked shop that's open 9am-5pm, 7 days a week; a food truck, open 10am–4pm; and an outdoor seating area in the courtyard. A B&B is also available on-site, and the site is a long-established venue for weddings and private events.

Tours: Yes, all year round. The tours are two hours long and run three to four times per day. Costing approximately £23pp, they can be booked in advance online and include tasting a wide range of wines, beers and liqueurs. No under-18s or dogs are permitted on the tours. Private tours and tastings are by appointment only.

Established: 1980

First Vintage Released: 1984

Size: 2 hectares

Grapes Grown: Bacchus, Madeleine Angevine, Regent

Annual Production:
30,000-35,000 bottles

Chiltern Valley is one of the long-established vineyards in the area, having been founded in 1980 when David Ealand, a maritime lawyer by profession, moved from London and bought Old Luxters, a pig farm in the Chiltern Hills. Soil analysis confirmed the chalk and clay east-facing slope was suitable for either rhubarb or grape vines and, one easy decision later, the first vines – mainly Reichensteiner – were planted in 1982.

Old Luxters Brewery was added to the site in 1990, around the same time weddings and other events became an important part of Chiltern Valley's portfolio. The site is well set up for visitors, with tours running all year, and is a popular destination for walkers and cyclists wanting to explore an official Area of Outstanding Natural Beauty.

CHILTERN VALLEY WINERY AND BREWERY

The vineyard is protected by warm air from an adjacent pond and tall trees that act as a windbreak. The border with Buckinghamshire lies just beyond the bottom of the vineyard. After 35 years, the Reichensteiner vines were replaced and only four rows of Regent remain from the original planting, alongside younger Bacchus and Madeleine Angevine. The estate wines produce around 2,000 bottles per year, with the yield increasing yearly and expected to reach around 5,000 bottles in the future. Fruit is also bought from other English vineyards and pressed and fermented in the winery, with the final range of wines and styles being heavily influenced by customer feedback. Pinot Noir grapes are bought in large quantities and the core range always comprises a dry white, a medium white, a rosé, and pink and white sparkling wines.

Very much family-run, David still lives on-site, and his three children are involved in the business, led by son Donald, who for many years was the production manager and is now a director. Jared, the winemaker, and Pawel, the brewer, carry out most of the day-to-day work, including all pruning, mowing and canopy management in the vineyard. The harvest is carried out by hand with help from a small team, including some of the part-time staff – mainly tour guides – and local volunteers.

The original two-tonne press is still used at harvest before fermentation in stainless steel tanks. Some wines, including red Pinot Noir and at least one white wine, use oak chips for additional flavour and body. The use of oak in sparkling wines can vary depending on the year and the blend. Grape skins, as well as spent hops from the brewery, are mulched back into the surrounding woodland.

The bottling and labelling is carried out in-house using an original state-of-the-art Italian bottling line. All wines are vegan, and the sparkling wines are aged on the lees for a minimum of 15 months before being disgorged.

Tours are very popular and include the brewery as well as the winery. The tasting room overlooks the Chiltern Hills and tastings are accompanied by cheese and crackers. Beers are bottle-conditioned and made with a variety of British hops including Fuggles, East Kent Goldings, Admiral & Olicana. There is B&B accommodation available, but booking in advance is recommended as the accommodation is included in the wedding packages – of which there are around 70 a year – so it is often fully booked on weekends. The converted 18th-century barn seats up to 114 people.

The attractive village of Hambleden, frequently used as a filming location, is just two miles away and is home to the Stag and Huntsman, which offers Chiltern Valley wines as well as accommodation. Henley itself lies around six miles south.

Brut

Vintage: Non-vintage   **ABV:** 12%

Grapes: Pinot Noir, Chardonnay

Typical Retail Price: £32

Nose: Sherbet with a hint of sweetness.

Palate: Rich, soft fruit, extremely fine mousse and creamy mouthfeel.

Comments: The wine spends a minimum 18 months on the lees.

Brut Rosé

Vintage: 2021   **ABV:** 12%

Grapes: Pinot Noir, Pinot Meunier

Typical Retail Price: £35

Nose: Chalky with red cherry.

Palate: Cherry fruit, a very smooth mouthfeel, and a hint of strawberry sweetness.

Comments: Made by the traditional method from Kentish fruit.

Chilli's Chiltern Dry

Vintage: 2022   **ABV:** 11%

Grapes: Madeleine Angevine, Reichensteiner

Typical Retail Price: £17

Nose: Aromatic and spicy.

Palate: Delicate floral, spice, and a smooth creamy finish.

Comments: Chilli is the name of the winery's fluffy, black cat – an excellent mouser.

Bacchus

Vintage: 2022 **ABV:** 11%

Grapes: Bacchus

Typical Retail Price: £18

Nose: Typical Bacchus nose; spicy and aromatic.

Palate: Fresh elderflower, light texture and a long, spicy finish.

Comments: Made with grapes from the adjacent vineyard.

Reichensteiner

Vintage: 2023 **ABV:** 11%

Grapes: Reichensteiner

Typical Retail Price: £18

Nose: Clean, subtly floral, and spicy.

Palate: Well-balanced and light with subtle tropical fruits and a gentle acidity.

Comments: A lovely, pale, clean and light wine.

Oaked Solaris

Vintage: 2023 **ABV:** 12%

Grapes: Solaris

Typical Retail Price: £19

Nose: Tangerine, oak and a nice, Riesling-like note of petrol.

Palate: Dry with delicate fig and lychee fruit, plus a gentle acidity that's underpinned by slightly sweet oak.

Comments: A pale gold colour and smooth texture.

DAWS HILL VINEYARD

Contact Details:
Town End Road,
Radnage,
Buckinghamshire, HP14 4DY
07833 462 597

What3Words:
///booth.sharpens.crystals

Website & Socials:
www.dawshillvineyard.co.uk
info@dawshillvineyard.co.uk
@dawshillvineyard

Visitor Centre:
The best way to visit is to book a tour or come to one of their events, such as a Blending Workshop or a Wine and Cheese Tasting in the winery's tasting area.

Tours:
Yes. 11am Saturdays during spring and summer, with additional tours occasionally available. Tours are two hours, £20pp, bookable online, and include tasting their current vintages. Private tours and events are available by appointment and come with an optional lunch.

Established: 2004

First Vintage Released: 2007

Size: 1.4 hectares

Grapes Grown: Chardonnay, Pinot Noir, Pinot Meunier, Auxerrois

Annual Production:
c 5,000 bottles

Daws Hill is nestled in the Chiltern Hills in Buckinghamshire, around four miles south-east of Chinnor and eight miles from Thame. Only sparkling wines are produced and, unusually for a vineyard of its size, all the wines are made on-site in the winery.

DAWS HILL VINEYARD

Daws Hill Vineyard was started as a retirement project by orthopaedic surgeon Nigel Morgan and his partner, Sarah, after they returned to Oxfordshire in 2003 following a period in France where they renovated houses. They were keen to bring back a piece of France with them, and Sarah's family home included stables that proved ideal for housing a winery. Nigel's daughter, Holly, is a free spirit who originally left England in 2009 to go travelling, but she would regularly return to help her father in the winter months. When Nigel passed away in 2016, Holly took over the running of the business which she now does with the help of friends, volunteers, and her partner Javier. Holly trained at Plumpton College in Sussex but is also grateful to the local winemakers who offered their time and advice during her early years heading the business.

The original planting comprised 3,000 vines of which Pinot Noir and Auxerrois were the majority. A further 2,000 Chardonnay and Pinot Noir vines were planted in 2007, making a total of 5,000. Around 30 volunteers help with pruning and harvesting, many of them working regularly in the vineyard for the love of being outside and close to nature. Even the original 2004 planting was carried out by volunteers, and Holly is always looking for more of them. Holly carries out mowing and spraying in the vineyard, which faces south and is steep enough at the top to cause some hairy moments when turning the tractor. The sloping vineyard is always around 2°c warmer than the rest of the site.

Pruned canes are composted and returned to the soil, which has less clay and is better drained than the rest of the site. Holly adopts a minimum intervention approach and notes how the local badgers keep away wasps and the local kites scare away smaller birds. Like many local vineyards, Daws Hill lost much of the 2020 crop due to late May frost, and the Auxerrois crop in 2023 was lost to mildew, but Holly is remarkably sanguine, observing that "you can't change the weather".

Wines are made in the traditional method and Holly aims to let the fruit express itself in the finished wines, although the exact blend of grapes varies from vintage to vintage. Acidity and sugar levels are monitored before harvesting, and once pressed, wines are fermented in stainless steel vessels. Holly now avoids malolactic fermentation, preferring sparkling wine styles with less butter and brioche character. After blending, the bottling is carried out by hand and then the wines are aged in the bottle for a minimum of three to four years. Riddling is also done by hand before disgorging and dosage. Sugar levels in the dosage are very low, and although Brut is declared on the labels, they are technically Extra Brut, with less than 6g of residual sugar per litre. Finally, the cork is added and the bottles are labelled, again by hand. No foil is added to the bottle; this is to prevent waste but has the added advantage of one less job to be done.

No fruit is bought or sold, and around 95% of the wines are sold directly to customers on-site or at farmers markets and other events, such as the Thame Food Festival and the Waddesdon Christmas Market. Duke's Wine Bar in Princes Risborough is also a regular stockist.

Auxerrois Blanc

Vintage: 2018 **ABV:** 12.5%

Grapes: Auxerrois Blanc

Typical Retail Price: £30

Nose: Green apple and bread.

Palate: Bready and dry with super-fine bubbles, a creamy texture, and long finish.

Comments: Auxerrois Blanc is used extensively in making Cremant d'Alsace.

Brut Rosé

Vintage: 2018 **ABV:** 11%

Grapes: Pinot Noir, Chardonnay, Pinot Meunier

Typical Retail Price: £30

Nose: Complex nose of redcurrants, rhubarb, and sherbet.

Palate: Tart red fruits balance a dry palate with plenty of mouthfeel and extremely fine bubbles.

Comments: A nice coppery pink colour and more lightly sparkling than similar wines. The blend is 80% Pinot Noir.

Sparkling Cider

Vintage: 2015 **ABV:** 7.5%

Grapes: N/A

Typical Retail Price: £15

Nose: Restrained cidery nose with a hint of liquorice.

Palate: Very clean, bone dry with subtle apple and a dry finish.

Comments: This elegant apple cider is made using the same traditional method as Daws Hill's wines and drinks more like a wine than a scrumpy. It would pair well with cheese, pork pie or asparagus.

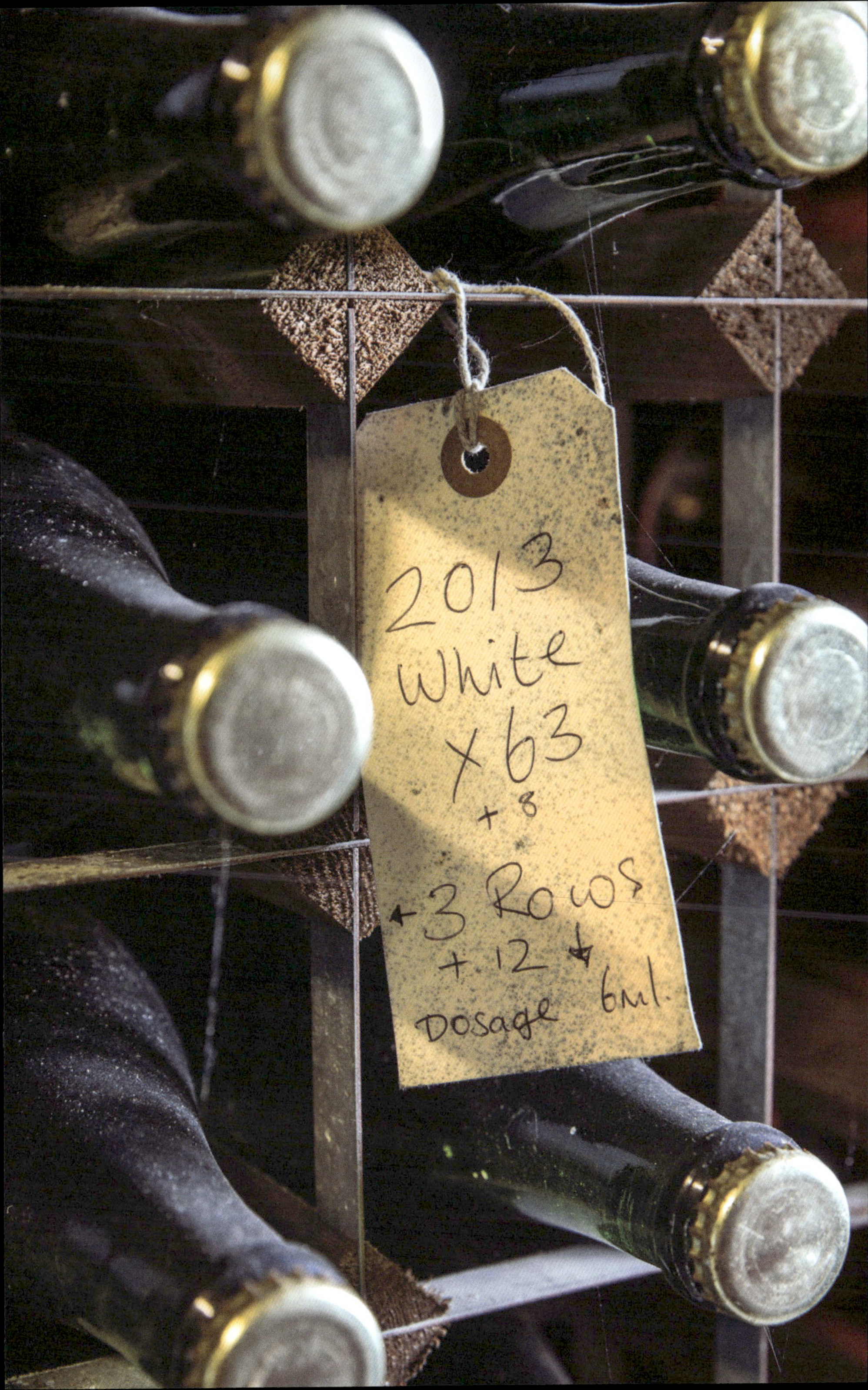
2013
White
x 63
+ 8
3 Rows
+ 12
6ml.
Dosage

FAIRMILE VINEYARD

Contact Details:

Fairmile,
Henley-on-Thames,
Oxfordshire, RG9 2LA
01491 598 588

What3Words:

///poems.gated.impeached

Website & Socials:

www.fairmilevineyard.co.uk
@fairmilevineyard
cheers@fairmilevineyard.co.uk

Visitor Centre:

No, but they welcome visitors on tours, tastings and tailor-made events that take place throughout the year. Visitors can also book a free slot and enjoy chilled wine and a picnic in the fully fenced vineyard. The lower part of the vineyard is wheelchair-accessible in dry weather, and the grounds are dog-friendly.

Tours:

Tour and tasting sessions are available by appointment from £15pp. Tours are one hour and run throughout the year. Visitors are also welcome to enjoy the grounds post-tour.

Established: 2012 (planted 2013)

First Vintage Released: 2015

Size: 3 hectares

Grapes Grown:

Chardonnay, Pinot Noir, Pinot Meunier

Annual Production:

c 20,000 bottles

Fairmile Vineyard is a producer of outstanding English sparkling wines and is conveniently located along the imposing Fairmile approach to Henley-on-Thames, within walking distance of the town centre and railway station.

Fairmile is a family affair, owned and run by Jan and Anthea Mirkowski. Anthea used to work in property while Jan, who had been making beer and wine at home for years, used to work in the corporate world of telecoms, specialising in environmental legislation. Having young children made the couple reassess their priorities, and they discovered Fairmile's site, which includes their family home, in 2011. The flinty, chalky soil, south-facing slope, and sub-100 metre altitude, reminiscent of the Champagne region, was ideal for sparkling wine production in England. Jan explains how the south-facing slope allows frost and water to run downhill, protecting the vines while maximising the grapes' exposure to the sun. The breeze from the Stonor Valley also helps to manage the vineyard's humidity and prevent mildew growth.

FAIRMILE VINEYARD

In the early years of Fairmile, legendary viticultural consultant Stephen Skelton MW was enlisted for his expertise and advice. The soil was prepared with a crop of winter mustard to improve the nitrogen content of the soil, then fertilised with compost from kitchen bin council collections. The site was fenced off to protect it from rabbits and deer, and in May 2013, 12,000 vines were planted in 12 hours using 13 GPS satellites to ensure their optimal positioning. Anthea now manages admin and finance in the office while Jan manages the vineyard.

Fairmile caused a minor sensation when its maiden 2015 vintage burst onto the scene in late 2018, immediately scooping an 'Outstanding' accolade from Decanter magazine. Since then, Jan says the wines have only improved, as more recent vintages are blended with mature reserves from previous years.

From the outset, Fairmile's vision was to exclusively make sparkling wines from classic Champagne varieties and to make them well. The proportion of each variety in the blends changes each year to ensure consistency. None of Fairmile's grapes are bought or sold.

Jan is proud of his vineyard management, taking meticulous care of pruning and showing off the worm casts that indicate good, healthy soil and the effective breakdown of leaves. Jan is highly respectful of the environment and chooses to maintain the existing mature trees on-site, despite the additional shade they give to some of the vines. These trees attract small birds and owls, while the site's lime trees provide homes for honeybees. Grass and wildflowers grow between the vine rows to encourage biodiversity.

Fairmile's harvest is done by hand thanks to locally recruited volunteers and professional vineyard workers. The wines are then made at the highly respected Hambledon Winery in Hampshire, using vegan-friendly clay-based finings to clear the wine. Their wines are available from the vineyard website, and at select times at their cellar door, as well as at wine merchants, farm shops, delicatessens, local Majestic stores, and fine-dining restaurants.

Looking to the future, Jan and Anthea have purchased an adjacent plot of land along the Fairmile slope, with the potential to double their annual production. They won't be rushed into further investment until the time is right, though; perhaps looking to their daughters to carry on the family legacy.

OXFORDSHIRE UNCORKED

Classic Cuvée

Vintage: Non-vintage   **ABV:** 12%

Grapes: Pinot Noir, Pinot Meunier, Chardonnay

Typical Retail Price: £35

Nose: Orchard fruits and buttered toast.

Palate: Zesty acidity, brittle mousse texture, leesy across the palate.

Comments: Notes taken from a Thames Valley and Chiltern Vineyards Association tasting and Fairmile's website.

Rosé

Vintage: Non-vintage   **ABV:** 12%

Grapes: Chardonnay, Pinot Noir, Pinot Meunier

Typical Retail Price: £39

Nose: Toast, rhubarb, and strawberry.

Palate: Bright cherry fruit with lovely, tart acidity.

Comments: The rosé is not oaked to keep it zingy and refreshing. Jan is very proud of the dark pink colour, hence the clear bottle. Store away from light.

Blanc de Blancs

Vintage: 2017   **ABV:** 12%

Grapes: Chardonnay

Typical Retail Price: £45

Nose: Delicate and appley with a hint of sweetness; reminiscent of apple crumble.

Palate: Light apple and lemon notes with a lovely, buttery hint, a very fine mousse, and a lingering fruity finish.

Comments: A delicious, subtle wine with a beguiling touch of sweetness that is extremely moreish. Matured on the lees for four years to provide complexity.

FREEDOM OF THE PRESS

Contact Details:
Ringwood Farm,
Minster Lovell,
Oxfordshire, OX29 0ND
07881 955 215

What3Words:
///basket.samplers.settle

Website & Socials:
www.freedomofthepress.co.uk
@freedomofthepresswinery
gavin@freedomofthepress.co.uk

Visitor Centre:
The winery is regularly open to the public from spring to summer, usually at the weekend when wine can be bought by the glass or bottle. Other occasional events, such as music recitals, are advertised on the winery's website.

Tours:
Yes, £20pp, taking place mainly on Saturdays from spring to summer. Tours last around one hour and include the tasting of three wines. Numbers are limited and tours must be booked in advance. Private tours and tastings are available by appointment.

Established: 2020

First Vintage Released: 2020

Size: N/A

Grapes Grown: N/A

Annual Production:
7,000-8,000 bottles

Most of the producers featured in this book own their vineyards and take their harvested fruit to a contract winery to be made into wine. Gavin Carver at Freedom of the Press, however, does the opposite. He buys the best fruit he can and makes his own wines at his winery.

Gavin lives in West Oxfordshire and has a background in theatre and academia, but also used to import wine, especially Burgundy, as a sideline business. In 2020, he cashed in his pension to indulge in his passion and Freedom of the Press was born. The site, situated just north of Minster Lovell on the edge of the Cotswolds, is distinctly rural, but its production of first-rate English wines follows a more urban ethos.

PINOT GRIS
2021

freedom of the press

75cl.

PARADOX
WHITE PINOT NOIR 2021

Initially, Gavin planned on setting up in Oxford, but Freedom's current site proved irresistible. John Worontschak of Litmus Wines was employed to provide winemaking expertise in the early years, giving Gavin time to immerse himself in research and learn all he could about the equipment and processes.

Gavin now describes himself as a "kit junkie" and takes great pride in his top-end equipment, optimising its use to create the best wines possible from the fruit available in each vintage. His high-tech yet gentle pump in the winery, for example, is the same model fisheries use to move live fish. To Gavin, winemaking is a form of alchemy, and his passion and knowledge is inspiring.

His wines are made with minimal intervention in what Gavin describes as a "classic style". The range of wines and how they are made differs yearly and depends on the quality of each vintage and the ripeness of the fruit. Gavin loves Pinot Noir, but he only makes a red wine in the best years – maybe one in every three or four. In cooler years, such as 2023, he uses the Pinot Noir to make rosé or white wines.

As well as ageing the wines on the lees, Gavin has a range of fermentation and maturation vessels at his disposal. From concrete to stoneware, and stainless steel to French oak barrels, he's careful to match the fruit to the right vessel to craft complex, food-friendly wines. The small-scale production allows him to monitor each batch and change vessels or blend them to achieve the perfect style. The Chardonnay and Pinot Noir tend to be oaked; the Pinot Gris is a blend of concrete and oak maturation; and stainless steel is used to make fresh, clean, fruity wines.

As well as the winery itself, stockists include the Oxford Wine Company, Daylesford, Eynsham Cellar, the Cellar Door in Oxford's Covered Market, and several local restaurants. Some wines are even exported to Norway, and in 2020, Freedom of the Press teamed up with Wood Brothers Distillery in Black Bourton to make a vermouth.

freedom
of the press

Chardonnay

Vintage: 2022   **ABV:** 13.5%

Grapes: Chardonnay

Typical Retail Price: £25

Nose: Delicate, floral and stone fruit.

Palate: Subtle and complex with a light buttery quality and good structure.

Comments: From a warm year, nicely balanced and will age well in the bottle for a couple of years.

Note, wine tasted prior to bottling, the photograph is of the 2021 vintage.

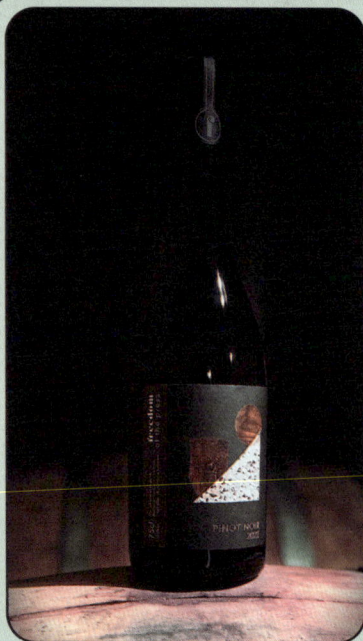

Pinot Noir

Vintage: 2022   **ABV:** 13.5%

Grapes: Pinot Noir

Typical Retail Price: £32

Nose: Red fruits.

Palate: Appetising, silky, red fruit with smoky, savoury notes and complexity.

Comments: Unfined to preserve its bold colour and only around 1,200 bottles made. This is a delicious red with ageing potential.

Pinot Noir Rosé

Vintage: 2023   **ABV:** 12%

Grapes: Pinot Noir

Typical Retail Price: £22 from the winery

Nose: Delicate floral notes, including fragrant rose petals.

Palate: Appetising fruitiness and earthiness with a notable texture and weight from six months' ageing on the lees.

Comments: Following a rather cool 2023, Gavin opted to make a rosé with his Pinot Noir grapes, which is blended from three Pinot Noir wines: one red, one rosé and one white. The result is an aromatic, complex and thoroughly enjoyable wine.

Note, wine tasted prior to bottling, the photograph is a 2020 vintage Rosé.

Pinot Gris

Vintage: 2021   **ABV:** 12.5%

Grapes: Pinot Gris

Typical Retail Price: £24

Nose: Pear and apricot with a hint of subtle oak.

Palate: Elegant, balanced, and structured with acidity, spice, and a long, dry finish.

Comments: Aged partly in concrete and partly in oak for complexity and weight. Do not over-chill to allow flavours to come out.

HARROW & HOPE

Contact Details:

Marlow Winery,
Pump Lane North,
Marlow, SL7 3RD
01628 481 091

What3Words:

///spend.swim.volunteered

Website & Socials:

www.harrowandhope.com
@harrowhope
enquiries@harrowandhope.com

Visitor Centre: Visits are made by appointment only. Purchases can be made from the cellar door and there's a tasting room which is used during tours.

Tours: Yes, on selected Wednesdays and Saturdays over the summer and occasional Fridays, too. Tours include tastings and a discount on any wines purchased. The tours sell out quickly, so should be booked well in advance. Pre-release days at the winery are advertised via H&H's mailing list. These usually take place on weekends and are a chance to tour the vineyard, taste wines, and secure new wines a couple of months before they are released.

Established: 2010

First Vintage Released: 2013

Size: 6.5 hectares

Grapes Grown:
Chardonnay, Pinot Noir, Pinot Meunier

Annual Production:
c 40,000 bottles

Just a few miles down the River Thames from Henley lies the attractive market town of Marlow in Buckinghamshire which, like Henley, sits at the foot of the Chiltern Hills. Harrow & Hope vineyard and winery sits less than two miles north of the centre, close to the long-established Rebellion Brewery. As well as being extremely close to Oxfordshire, Harrow & Hope makes wines for two of Oxfordshire's vineyards: Wyfold and Kidmore.

Harrow & Hope is run by Henry and Kaye Laithwaite of the famous wine family. They met at university while studying biology and later married and moved to France in 2009 where Henry bought fruit and made wines in Côtes de Castillon, Bordeaux. After some time, the couple began to miss England and Henry wanted to gain control of the winemaking process from farm to bottle. So, they looked for a suitably chalky site with good drainage for making sparkling wines and found their current site in 2010, planting three hectares of vines the same year. Another three hectares were planted in 2012, making a total proportion of 40% Chardonnay, 40% Pinot Noir and 20% Pinot Meunier. Much of their crop uses clones from France grafted onto US root stocks. The site's south-facing slope has maximum exposure to the sun and the flinty soil provides good drainage while radiating additional heat to the vines. The chalk levels vary across the site and the Pinot Noir vines enjoy additional moisture from the clay content in the soil at the top of the slope.

The downside of the flinty soil is that it was a "nightmare" to cultivate, according to Kaye. More positively, it also gave rise to the winery's name as, during planting, they harrowed the land and hoped for the best, breaking various bits of equipment during the process.

The vineyard has been farmed organically since 2020 and received Soil Association certification in 2023. Agronomist John Buchan helped Henry and Kaye to set up the vineyard, with additional help from Mike, Tamara and Simon Roberts from Ridgeview in Sussex. The team worked, and continue to work hard, to select the best cover crops for the soil and the vines. No additional fruit is bought, and none is sold either. In the vineyard, the focus is on minimal intervention and allowing the fruit to express terroir, concentrating on quality rather than yield. Henry, Kaye and their small team do all the pruning, bud-rubbing and harvesting. Manure from local farms is used in addition to the vineyard's own compost.

In 2016, 65% of the potential harvest was lost to frost. Now, candles are used to protect the crop in April, and the team is on standby for when the temperature drops below 2°c. During the harvest, the four-tonne press is used intensively, with multiple presses per day, every day, for three weeks or more. Then, small tanks and French oak casks are used to vinify the different clones of each variety, giving Henry and assistant winemaker James maximum options for ageing and blending the wines. Additionally, wild yeasts are used during fermentation.

When they first planted, Tony Jordan, Moët & Chandon's legendary winemaker who developed Moët's Australian and other overseas operations, visited Harrow & Hope regularly and helped Henry to improve his knowledge of, and techniques for, making sparkling wine. Henry continually talks about trying new things and observing the results. He now has good stocks of reserve wines which can be used for making exciting new blends as well as ensuring consistency, where needed, and complexity from one year to the next.

Their assistant winemaker, James, was trained at Plumpton College and in Tuscany and South Africa; he shares Henry's passion for discovery and experimentation, and the two of them talk excitedly about making English wines without some of the restrictions imposed by France's strict appellation definitions. One can't help but share in their excitement for discovering what's possible for English wine.

Brut Reserve No.8

Vintage: Non-vintage   **ABV:** 12%

Grapes: Pinot Noir, Chardonnay, Pinot Meunier

Typical Retail Price: £33

Nose: Toast and cherries.

Palate: Clean with bright acidity, structure and a long finish.

Comments: Although non-vintage, the No.8 label indicates the base year was a 2019 vintage (for the majority of the blend). Significant quantities of older vintage wines, some lightly oaked, provide complexity and mouthfeel. Note, image is for a later vintage. The blend is 40% Pinot Noir, 40% Chardonnay, and 20% Pinot Meunier.

Blanc de Noirs

Vintage: 2019   **ABV:** 12%

Grapes: Pinot Noir

Typical Retail Price: £42

Nose: Subtle berries and a hint of marzipan.

Palate: Elegant, subtle and complex with creamy mouthfeel.

Comments: 50% of the wine was fermented in oak barrels, giving both mouthfeel and length, and a minimum of three and a half years on the lees adds further complexity. This is one of Harrow & Hope's flagship wines. Note, image is for a later vintage.

Blanc de Blancs

Vintage: 2018   **ABV:** 12%

Grapes: Chardonnay

Typical Retail Price: £40

Nose: Complex apples and toast.

Palate: Smooth texture with very fine bubbles, tart fruit, a hint of sweetness and a long, moreish finish.

Comments: Its complexity comes from barrel ageing and three years on the lees. Note, image is for a later vintage

HENDRED VINEYARD

Contact Details:
Allins Lane,
East Hendred, Wantage,
Oxfordshire OX12 8HR
01235 834 770

What3Words:
///explained.bottled.optimists

Website & Socials:
www.hendredvineyard.co.uk
@hendred_vineyard
info@hendredvineyard.co.uk

Visitor Centre:
Advance appointments are required
for the shop. Bottles can be purchased
online and collected from the shop.
Occasional open days take place in
summer and are advertised on their
website and social media.

Tours:
By appointment only.

Established: 1972

First Vintage Current Owners:
2014

Size: 1.4 hectares

Grapes Grown:
Pinot Noir, Seyval Blanc, Madeleine
Angevine, Bacchus

Annual Production:
6,000-10,000 bottles

One of Oxfordshire's long-standing vineyards, Hendred was first planted by the McKinnon family in the early 1970s, then bought and managed by the Callaghans between 2006 and 2013. The exact area planted with vines has fluctuated over the years, as have the varieties grown; under previous owners, wines were even made on the premises.

In 2014, Eileen and David Bell, both wine lovers who lived in the village, purchased the vineyard where they now live with their family. They continue to be mindful of the role the vineyard plays in the village and its community. The current vineyard is 1.4 hectares and only uses the best, non-shaded areas of the south-facing plot. Bacchus was planted in 2021 with the first crop in 2024. In time, this should increase total production to around 10,000 bottles per annum. Around 90% of its current production is sold within a five-mile radius of the vineyard, and each year's release sells out within the year.

HENDRED VINEYARD

Eileen is of farming ancestry and manages the commercial and marketing side of the business. David's on-going finance career involves investing in small companies, much like Hendred Vineyard, but he also carries out much of the work in the vineyard, including mowing and weeding. The couple are assisted by two friends: Biagio Grillo and Phillipe Desaint. Originally from Sicily, Biago is now in his 80s and helped to plant many of the existing vines back in the 1990s. Philippe, himself from France, provides expertise and helps with regular work in the vineyard, including pruning and canopy management.

The vineyard is on chalk soil with clay sides and is well drained with a gentle westerly slope running down to a brook. All varieties use a double Guyot system with trunks pruned low to the ground. Around 35% of the vines are Pinot Noir, 25% Seyval Blanc and 20% each of Bacchus and Madeleine Angevine.

David notes wryly that most English vineyards tend to be susceptible to either frost or mildew and, in Hendred's case, the biggest problem has been frost. It was no coincidence to them that their first frost-free year produced three times as much fruit. Having tried multiple ways to combat the frost, Eileen and David now run an intriguing system, using a solar-powered pump. The pump takes water from their on-site pond and distributes it to efficient, pulsing spray heads positioned amongst the trellises that spray water over the vines in freezing temperatures. Because freezing water emits a small amount of heat energy, the ice forming on the vines stays constant at around 0°c, even when surrounding temperatures are lower, and this ice protects the young buds and shoots from damage.

This is just one way that the Bells try to be sustainable and sensitive to the natural environment around them. There are no deer fences around the vineyard – although, thankfully, the local muntjacs seem to prefer apples to grapes – and Eileen, who loves nature, uses cameras to record visits from owls, otters, badgers and roe deer, amongst others.

Hendred's wines are produced at Three Choirs in Gloucestershire. Sugar and acidity are monitored before harvest, and then the harvest itself – an enjoyable day which is often oversubscribed – is carried out by local volunteers. Eileen and David aim to make consistent, quality wines, both still and sparkling, although the exact line-up is not decided until after harvest. Around 50% of production is sparkling and is made using the traditional method, with dosages kept low in sugar and the wines dry. This may fall to 30% once the Bacchus is fully established and more varietal still wines can be produced.

In the village nearby, The Eyston Arms and Wheatsheaf pubs occasionally take Hendred wines for events. Their regular stockists include the village shop, Millets Farm in Frilford, and the nearby Q Gardens Farm Shop.

...yard.

...PEN

...ay 9 June

...- 5 pm

...ines !

Hendred Brut

Vintage: 2018 (Not declared) **ABV:** 12%

Grapes: Pinot Noir, Seyval Blanc

Typical Retail Price: £23

Nose: Chalky, sherbet, pear and brioche.

Palate: Rich and long with pear, apple and blackberries.

Comments: Matured on the lees for three years.

Hendred Brut Rosé

Vintage: 2020 (not declared) **ABV:** 12%

Grapes: Pinot Noir, Seyval Blanc

Typical Retail Price: £23

Nose: Chalky, red berries and hint of spice.

Palate: Lots of fine fizz, lovely acidity, a soft mouthfeel and good length.

Comments: A pale salmon fizz that was aged on the lees for two years yet is light and refreshing.

Hendred Spring

Vintage: 2022　　**ABV:** 11%

Grapes: Madeleine Angevine, Seyval Blanc

Typical Retail Price: £12

Nose: Floral, spicy and Riesling-like.

Palate: Citrusy and herbaceous with good acidity and plenty of length.

Comments: A good example of two varieties working well together.

Hendred Rosé

Vintage: 2022　　**ABV:** 11%

Grapes: Pinot Noir, Seyval Blanc

Typical Retail Price: £13

Nose: Chalky, strawberry.

Palate: Fresh, floral and bone-dry.

Comments: Salmon coloured, refreshing, and winner of Best Rosé in recent regional competitions; the 2023 vintage is 100% Pinot Noir.

JOJO'S VINEYARD

Contact Details:

Russells Water,
Henley-on-Thames,
Oxfordshire, RG9 6EU
07967 637 985

What3Words:

///spare.wonderfully.configure

Website & Socials:

www.jojosvineyard.co.uk
@jojos_vineyard
hello@jojosvineyard.co.uk

Visitor Centre:

No, but planning permission has been granted with a likely opening in 2025. Until then, pre-booked tours, tastings, and other events are hosted in marquees by the vineyard, and wine is available to purchase.

Tours:

By appointment only, and tours can include an optional picnic board to be enjoyed on the grounds.

Established: 2019

First Vintage Released: 2021

Size: 2.2 hectares

Grapes Grown:

Chardonnay, Pinot Noir, Pinot Meunier, Pinot Blanc, Bacchus, Seyval Blanc, Frühburgunder (Précoce)

Annual Production:

6,000-10,000 bottles

JoJo's is a relative newcomer with an exciting future. It's owned and run by husband-and-wife team Ian and Tess Beecher-Jones, and it's named after their free-spirited dog, JoJo. After ten years of living in the village of Russells Water, near Henley in the Chiltern Hills, they purchased a neighbouring plot of land in 2016. Two years of hard graft followed, where they readied the soil before planting around 9,000 vines in 2019. The vineyard is on a south-westerly Chiltern slope and offers glorious views of rural Oxfordshire.

Ian and Tess enlisted the help of expert Ed Mitcham to set up the fledgling vineyard, and he continues to provide support and advice. Ed learnt his trade in New Zealand and runs Yew Tree Vineyard in West Hagbourne, Oxfordshire. Yew Tree's wines are not commercially available; the vineyard sells its fruit to other wineries.

Tess's day job is in pharmaceutical R&D and Ian's is in precision agriculture. Together, they combine Tess's scientific thinking and passion for wine with Ian's land and viticulture expertise to create fine English wines. As part of Ian's job, he helps design and sell high-tech machinery to wine producers around the world. He sees technical innovation, such as digital data capture, as the way forward in improving vineyard management and wine quality. His enthusiasm is infectious, and he enjoys selling British technology to vineyards in more established wine-producing countries. He co-invented the S-Rex direct drill with a neighbouring vineyard manager, which is designed to plant multiple soil-enriching plants between the vines in a single pass, improving the soil while reducing fuel and labour. Robots and drones travel between and above JoJo's vines, mowing the plants in between the rows, assessing vine health, assisting pickers in collecting fruit efficiently, and creating yield maps of the vineyard. Capturing data across the vineyard, Ian believes, improves decision-making and the production process. JoJo's blend of new and traditional wine growing techniques is a core component in their production of the highest quality grapes.

Despite JoJo's passion for harnessing technology, the wines are made with minimum intervention by Andy Wiles and head winemaker Tommy Grimshaw at the Langham Estate in Dorset. JoJo's focus is on quality over quantity, and their careful bunch selection - carried out by hand using friends, family and local volunteers - ensures only the best and ripest grapes are harvested. Tommy works closely with JoJo's to create wines with a distinctive style. Their wines are unfiltered and wild yeasts are used in fermentation. They are aged in a mixture of oak barrels and stainless steel to allow layers of flavour to develop naturally.

JoJo's first release, 2021's Bacchus/Seyval Blanc blend, is delightfully ethereal and provides a tantalising glimpse into what will be their first release of traditional method sparkling wines. These will include a Cuvée Classic, made with the three Champagne grape varieties and Pinot Blanc, and a rich-style Rosé Elegance made from Pinot Noir, Seyval Blanc and Frühburgunder (an early-ripening variety of Pinot Noir, also know as Précoce).

Bacchus/Seyval Blanc

Vintage: 2021 **ABV:** 11%

Grapes: Bacchus, Seyval Blanc

Typical Retail Price: £22

Nose: Delicate, with hints of lemon and elderflower.

Palate: Light, clean and elegant with delightful acidity and notes of elderflower, lemon and apple. A brief period of oak-ageing provides structure, and a long, dry finish makes this a very appetising and attractive wine.

Comments: Subtle, elegant and elusive, this wine is deliciously drinkable. The blend of the wine will change each year to maintain freshness and subtlety; the 2021 vintage contains 26% Seyval Blanc while the 2022 contains 15%.

KIDMORE ORGANIC VINEYARD

Contact Details:

Chalkhouse Green Road,
Kidmore End,
Oxfordshire RG4 9AR
07818 011 690

What3Words:

///loopholes.chopper.reservoir

Website & Socials:

www.kidmorevineyard.com

@kidmore_vineyard

stephen@kidmorevineyard.com

Visitor Centre:

No, but there are plans to host visitors and events once their wines are released.

Tours:

Not yet, but the garden and vineyard often participates in National Garden Scheme open days which can be booked online.

Established: 2018

First Vintage Released: 2022, pending release in 2027

Size: 1 hectare

Grapes Grown:

Chardonnay, Pinot Noir, Pinot Meunier

Annual Production:

c 6,000 bottles

Stephen and Niamh Kendall moved to Kidmore House, near Sonning Common, in 2002. Kidmore House has a long and fascinating history dating back to 1158. The current house was built around 1680 and is Grade II* listed. During the 20th century, the house was owned by Major Huguenot Waterhouse and Lady Caroline Waterhouse, the second daughter of the 10th Duke of Marlborough, and thus relatives Sir Winston and Lady Churchill were regular visitors.

Stephen used to have a career in banking and technology and Niamh is a trained horticulturist (a profession that runs in the family). They have long been wine enthusiasts, touring France regularly, and so planting the one-hectare vineyard on the estate in 2018 felt like a natural step. From the start, they knew they wanted to farm the vineyard organically, and it is now fully certified by The Soil Association.

KIDMORE ORGANIC VINEYARD

Vineyard-owning friends in Sussex advised Stephen and Niamh that their south-facing site, with its well-drained, sandy loam soil and valley breeze, was perfect for vines. Ed Mitchum, the local vineyard expert, advises Kidmore and helps the vineyard reach its full potential; Ed and his team also help with the harvest. The first harvest, in 2022, produced 1,500 bottles, but the second, from the bumper 2023 crop, yielded 6,500.

Stephen loves French wines and when he describes rich, luscious Champagne styles, it's easy to see what sort of sparkling wines he hopes to produce at Kidmore. Ageing bottle-fermented wines on the lees adds weight, mouthfeel and complexity, and Stephen is in no hurry to release wines until they are at their best; four to five years from harvest to release is most likely, although Stephen describes the wines from the first tastings as already delicious.

The vines use a single Guyot system and are planted one metre apart to limit vigour and maximise quality. Winter pruning is carried out by Ed Mitcham's team, and the pruned canes are mulched and returned to the vineyard. Guest sheep help keep the weeds down in the winter, candles prevent spring frost damage, and Stephen continuously manages spraying, wire-lifting, and the vine canopy throughout the summer. The 4,500 vines are 50% Chardonnay, 35% Pinot Noir and 15% Pinot Meunier.

Although there are no facilities for visitors or tours yet, Kidmore House's garden and vineyard regularly take part in the National Garden Scheme which opens private gardens to the public on specific days (see the NGS website for details). As well as the vineyard, visitors can see some 50-year-old vines within the walled garden which are not used for production, but that can be good early indicators of disease.

Kidmore's wines are made by Henry Laithwaite at Harrow & Hope in Marlow and are certified organic. Stephen and Niamh consider farming the vineyard sustainably and organically to be a natural and logical choice, and they are already exploring sustainable bottle options made from recycled glass. The initial line-up of wines will include a sparkling white and sparkling rosé, initially vintage only, but all blending options are considered given the individual year's harvest quality. The labels and design work are in the early stages but, like the wines, will be distinctive and characterful.

Once the wines are released, there are plans for a three-bedroom barn conversion to provide visitor accommodation. Tours, events, and a designated tasting room are also likely to be introduced. With a glint in his eye, Stephen explains he is already considering planting a second hectare on the land adjacent to their first hectare. The future looks exciting for Kidmore, and the release of their first wines will be cause for celebration indeed.

LITTLE OAK VINEYARD

Contact Details:
Paxford Road,
Chipping Campden,
Gloucestershire GL55 6LA
07812 339 556

What3Words:
///likewise.potential.fidgeted

Website & Socials:
www.littleoakvineyard.com
@littleoakvineyard
admin@littleoakvineyard.com

Visitor Centre: Bottles can be purchased online. Private events and parties are hosted in a marquee amongst the vines in the summer. Otherwise, the best way to visit is to book a tour.

Tours: Year-round, Wednesday-Sunday at 11am, and booking is required. Occasionally, afternoon tours are available in the summer, with both the tour and tasting taking place outside. In winter and poorer weather, there is a presentation and tasting indoors. Tours are £25pp including tasting. Private tours and events are by appointment only.

Established: 2005

First Vintage Released: 2009

Size: 1.5 hectares

Grapes Grown:
Siegerrebe, Seyval Blanc, Divico

Annual Production:
8,000-10,000 bottles

Little Oak Vineyard was conceived by owner Steve Wilson during the hot summers of 2004 and 2005. His one-hectare meadow, previously used for horses, sloped gently from north to south, and Steve tested several varieties before deciding Siegerrebe was the most suitable and planting 300 vines in 2006. The first harvest, in 2009, yielded a total of six bottles which were consumed joyously with friends on the very evening they arrived from the winery.

LITTLE OAK VINEYARD

The vineyard has a sandy silt loam soil with good drainage. Steve received help and advice from nearby Three Choirs Vineyard and planted additional Siegerrebe and Seyval Blanc vines using a Geneva Double Curtain (GDC) training system: this means the vines try to grow across the alleys between the rows, often creating a large canopy which needs careful pruning to let in sunlight. Little Oak's first sparkling wine was made from the 2014 Seyval harvest, and their 2016 vintage won a medal at the 2019 Decanter World Wine Awards. Steve favours a dry, crisp style with good acidity, and so harvests as soon as there is enough sugar in the grapes to make wine. This results in fully fermented wines with a relatively low alcohol content, typically 10.5% to 11.5%. The white and sparkling wines are fermented in stainless steel, without oak.

In 2022, an adjacent plot of land was purchased. This was planted with Divico in 2023, a Swiss grape of Gamay ancestry, bringing the total hectarage to nearly 1.5. Steve is excited about the opportunities this will provide, with 60 test vines from 2021 fruiting a year earlier than expected and providing a potential increase in annual production of approximately 5,000 bottles.

Little Oak is very much a family business. Gemma, Steve's wife, manages the tours and the day-to-day running of the vineyard with the help of her children. Pruning is done by the family, and Steve describes how the secateurs have become an extension of his body, like a good pair of shoes. Around 20 local students and volunteers help with harvest, as do the chickens which roam freely around the vineyard.

Steve and Gemma are passionate about producing a quality product. Sulphites have always been kept to a minimum and the wines are vegan. The 2014 vintage of Siegerrebe was considered inadequate, with Steve explaining "there was no sunshine in the bottle", and was thus made into brandy instead. This proved so successful that brandy continues to be made at nearby Charles Martell & Son distillery when the harvest is plentiful enough. Beyond wine, Steve also enjoys making cider and marmalade from Little Oak's fruit trees.

Little Oak also offers a vine leasing package which includes an annual tasting event, discounts, and an allowance of wine in return for an annual fee. The vineyard is only one mile from the beautiful village of Chipping Campden, which has plentiful accommodation and is home to Fillet & Bone Farm Shop, which stocks Little Oak wines along with many other local food and drink producers. The Little Oak website lists local taxis and accommodation suggestions.

Little Oak Sparkling White

Vintage: 2019   **ABV:** 12%

Grapes: Seyval Blanc

Typical Retail Price: £29

Nose: Subtle, chalky and yeasty.

Palate: Clean and elegant with fine bubbles, bright acidity, and notes of lemon and sherbet.

Comments: Made using the traditional bottle-fermented method. Brut in style with a small amount of Siegerrebe added in the dosage.

Siegerrebe

Vintage: 2022   **ABV:** 10.5%

Grapes: Siegerrebe

Typical Retail Price: £16

Nose: Elderflower and spice.

Palate: Clean with light body, appetising acidity, and hints of herb and spice.

Comments: Crisper and drier than the 2021 vintage; Steve delights in how the characteristics vary from one vintage to another.

Row 9

OAKEN GROVE VINEYARD

Contact Details:
Benhams Lane,
Fawley, Henley-on-Thames,
Oxon, RG9 6JG
07792 633 987

What3Words:
///uptake.lakes.tastings

Website & Socials:
www.oakengrovevineyard.co.uk
@oakengrovevineyard
info@oakengrovevineyard.co.uk

Visitor Centre: Yes: a cellar door, shop and covered wine terrace overlooking the vineyard are open Fridays and Saturdays in spring and summer, and wine is available by the glass or bottle from their homely bar. Platters of local cheeses and charcuterie can be ordered in advance. There is an attractive events room which can be hired for private or corporate events, and they also host jazz evenings and other events year-round.

Tours: Two two-hour tours per day on Saturdays, March to October. £25pp including wine tastings of two sparkling and three still wines. Optional platters are available and can be booked online or in person on arrival. Private tours of 12 or more can be arranged by appointment. They hope to expand their tour offerings in future.

Established: 1986, replanted 2005

First Vintage new planting: 2009

Size: 3 hectares

Grapes Grown: Bacchus, Pinot Noir, Madeleine Angevine, Reichensteiner

Annual Production:
10,000-15,000 bottles

Oaken Grove Vineyard is located up a steep, wooded lane just three miles from the centre of Henley-on-Thames. Owner Phil Rossi jokes that the vineyard is too large to be a hobby, but too small to be commercial. Running Oaken Grove is clearly a labour of love for Phil, who has been involved since it was established by his mother in 1986.

OAKEN GROVE VINEYARD

Phil left school and travelled to Tasmania when he was sixteen, where he attended further education colleges and worked in vineyards. He likens English wine production to that of Tasmania: once snubbed, but now harnessing its cooler climate to produce critically acclaimed wines. When he returned to England, Phil took on the management of the vineyard and has made it into the welcoming venue it is today. Some of the original Bacchus vines are still producing fruit, but most of the vineyard was re-planted between 2005 and 2007. Phil knew he wanted to continue producing still wines, so he planted 6,000 vines accordingly, but he continues to review the optimal mix of varieties.

Until recently, Phil effectively held down two full-time jobs, but in 2018 he left a career in retail design and management to focus on the vineyard and its visitor centre. Phil has a deep love of nature and aims to make the best quality wine with the smallest environmental impact. The chickens on-site wander freely around the vineyard, and Oaken Grove is one of six sites hosting beehives for local producer Honeys of Henley. Foil or PVC bottle tops have been axed, seen as unnecessary waste, and empty wine bottles are reused and sold as candles, with their corks also being recycled.

Phil does most of the pruning himself, finding it useful to assess the health of the vines and set them up well for the next season. Leaf-stripping is also done by hand, and Phil favours UV light to prevent fungus growth. The original wide spacing between the vine rows has been kept so the wind can penetrate and pollinate the vines, maximising the potential ripening of the grapes. The harvest is carried out by hand with the help of around 20 wine lovers, customers, friends and family.

The wines are then made at a local state-of-the-art winery. The range varies from year to year depending on the harvest and uses the best options from the grapes grown that year. Red Pinot Noir is made from warmer vintages only. In 2023, the Bacchus harvest was large enough to make a sparkling Bacchus, to be released in 2025. Benham Blush, between vintages at time of writing, is a rosé wine made from Pinot Noir and is one of Oaken Grove's most popular wines. No additional fruit is bought, so most vintages sell out each year.

The attractive wine terrace and events space are relatively recent additions to Oaken Grove, and it's difficult to imagine a more pleasant location to enjoy a cheese platter from local producers like Nettlebed Creamery. Sterl, who runs most of the vineyard tours, is incredibly passionate about visitor experience and is always keen to welcome guests back to Oaken Grove.

Embers, a high-end campsite, and Greenlands Hotel are both within walking distance of Oaken Grove. Danesfield House Hotel is a short taxi ride away, whilst Henley has plenty of accommodation options including an Hotel du Vin. Buses from Henley stop at the bottom of Benhams Lane, less than a mile from the vineyard.

Rosé de Noirs

Vintage: 2019   **ABV:** 11.5%

Grapes: Pinot Noir

Typical Retail Price: £35

Nose: Delicately floral.

Palate: Delightfully refreshing with subtle citrus notes and a fine mousse.

Comments: Around 2,500 bottles were made; the colour is exceptionally light for a rosé.

Bacchus

Vintage: 2020   **ABV:** 11.5%

Grapes: Bacchus

Typical Retail Price: £17

Nose: Elderflower.

Palate: Subtle and bright with a crisp finish akin to Riesling.

Comments: Very light colour; no oak.

Benhams Orchard

Vintage: 2022 **ABV:** 11%

Grapes: Reichensteiner, Madeleine Angevine

Typical Retail Price: £17

Nose: Floral with a hint of vanilla.

Palate: Clean, appley fruitiness.

Comments: Fermented with a light use of oak chips to maintain the brightness of fruit.

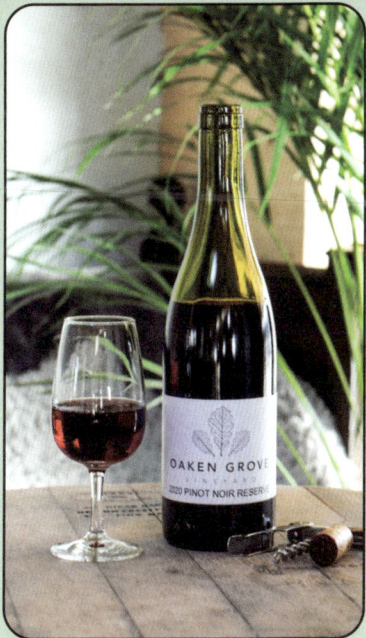

Pinot Noir Reserve

Vintage: 2020 **ABV:** 11.5%

Grapes: Pinot Noir

Typical Retail Price: £25

Nose: Delicate hint of red fruits.

Palate: Complex with appealing blackcurrant fruit. Good structure and a eucalyptus finish.

Comments: Oaken Grove vowed to only make a red if it was going to be excellent, and this red – their first - is from the warm 2020 vintage that was harvested well into October. Decanting will help bring out the flavours, and the wine has ageing potential.

POULTON HILL

Contact Details:
Poulton,
Cirencester GL7 5JA
01285 850 257

What3Words:
///kilowatt.dozen.press

Website & Socials:
www.poultonhillestate.co.uk
@poultonhillestate
info@poultonhillestate.co.uk

Visitor Centre: Yes, and the cellar door is open year-round, Tuesday-Friday, 9-5pm and Saturday, 11-3pm. Summer opening hours may be longer, and wine is sold by the glass as well as by the bottle. Special events take place every summer.

Tours: Tours run for an hour and a half at £25pp and include the tasting of four wines. They start at 11am (and 2pm on Saturdays), and booking is advised as spaces are limited to 20 people per tour. A tasting-only option is also available in the winter months, and private tours can be arranged by appointment. The Long Room, for private events, and the luxury Country House accommodation are both available for hire.

Established: 2010

First Vintage Released: 2012

Size: 3 hectares

Grapes Grown:
Phoenix, Seyval Blanc, Bacchus, Regent, Rondo, Pinot Noir

Annual Production: c 15,000 bottles

Poulton Hill is nestled close to Cirencester, on the edge of the Cotswolds, and boasts a proactive approach to welcoming visitors year-round.

Originally planted as a hobby by the estate's owner, the 10,000-vine vineyard is now run by a small team led by Natalie and Diogo. Virtually everything is managed by hand, from pruning and bud-rubbing to marketing, labelling and deliveries. Natalie has previously worked for Laithwaites as well as vineyards in Australia, New Zealand and Bordeaux; the meticulous Diogo, who is a key part of the estate team, worked in French vineyards during his teens.

POULTON HILL

The vineyard is on a south-facing slope with clay soil that retains moisture, meaning watering the vines has only been necessary once. Italian alder trees act as windbreakers and the vineyard is frequently visited by hares, partridges and woodpeckers. A flock of Babydoll sheep keep the spaces between the vines tidy and trimmed.

The white grapes - Phoenix, Seyval and Bacchus - are planted in similar proportions and account for around 70% of the vines. The vigorous and high-yielding Phoenix requires frequent leaf stripping to keep its canopy clear and let in the sunlight. Poulton's red varieties are particularly popular with birds so are sometimes netted to protect the crop. The fruit is also trained on high wires to safeguard against mildew, although careful monitoring is also required. In the winter, candles are used to prevent frost damage after the critical budding stage.

Most of the vines are from the original planting, with Pinot Noir being added in 2018. Pinot Noir vines are trained with a single arm to concentrate the fruit, which is then used in sparkling and rosé wines. Since 2015, their sparkling wines have been branded 'Bulari', which is a derivative of the Latin 'Bullarum', meaning bubbles - a fitting name given Poulton Hill's proximity to Roman Cirencester.

Towards the end of summer and before the harvest, the grapes are tested regularly for their sugar content and acidity. The harvest is then carried out by hand with around 15 local volunteers helping per day. While Natalie manages the volunteer database, Diogo's wife provides the volunteers with a much needed and gratefully received lunch on harvest days.

Poulton's wines are made at Three Choirs in Gloucestershire – one of the largest and oldest producers in England – and the Poulton Hill team use the facilities there to decide the exact blends. Their sparkling wines are made by the traditional method and are disgorged 500 bottles at a time, meaning some bottles benefit from extended maturation. Their sparkling wines are from a single vintage and all of them are vegan.

Looking to the future of Poulton Hill, there are hopes for additional plantings on the estate, increased numbers within the team, and further event offerings. They recently launched events in June, including a pop-up pizza van, and this will continue every Friday throughout the summer (with different pop-up food trucks) until at least mid-September.

Stockists include Burford Garden Company, Jesse Smith Butchers, Jolly Nice Farmshop, local Co-op supermarkets, and Poulton Hill's sister company, Bibury Trout Farm. A wholesaler is also employed, making Poulton Hill wines available across the UK. As well as their wines, they produce a spirit from hand-picked sloe berries, Sloe de Vie, as well as a triple-distilled Cotswold brandy and a vermouth.

Bulari Brut

Vintage: 2019 **ABV:** 11.5%

Grapes: Seyval Blanc, Pinot Noir

Typical Retail Price: £39

Nose: Green apple and elderflower.

Palate: Clean with green apple, a fine mousse and a lemon sherbet finish.

Comments: Surprisingly golden in appearance, this is a pleasant, crisp and easy-drinking sparkling wine with a production of around 2,000-2,500 bottles per year. Its 2018 crop was a medal winner at the Wine GB Awards in 2022.

Rosé Brut

Vintage: Non-vintage **ABV:** 11.5%

Grapes: Seyval Blanc, Rondo

Typical Retail Price: £38

Nose: Gentle rose petal and citrus.

Palate: Refreshing and racy, with lemon citrus, red cherry and sherbet.

Comments: Light in texture but with a lengthy sherbet finish. The blend is 65% Seyval Blanc and 35% Rondo.

Arlington White

Vintage: 2022 **ABV:** 11%

Grapes: Phoenix, Seyval Blanc

Typical Retail Price: £19

Nose: Herbaceous nose from the Phoenix grapes and a hint of sweetness.

Palate: Appley sweetness with balanced acidity and a light body.

Comments: An off-dry wine made following demand from customers. Named after the famous Arlington cottages in Bibury. The blend is around 60% Phoenix and 40% Seyval Blanc.

Phoenix

Vintage: 2022 **ABV:** 11.5%

Grapes: Phoenix, Seyval Blanc

Typical Retail Price: £19

Nose: Delicate grapefruit and green apple.

Palate: Clean with bright acidity and a grapefruit finish.

Comments: Although declared as Phoenix, 15% Seyval Blanc is added. Do not overchill to allow the flavours to come out.

Rosé

Vintage: 2022 **ABV:** 11%

Grapes: Phoenix, Pinot Noir, Seyval

Typical Retail Price: £19

Nose: Herbaceous and floral.

Palate: Plenty of refreshing acidity, a light body, and hints of summer fruits.

Comments: The appetising salmon-pink colour comes from less than two hours of contact with the skins after crushing; a refreshing wine made for summer enjoyment.

Arlington Red

Vintage: Non-vintage **ABV:** 11.5%

Grapes: Regent, Rondo

Typical Retail Price: £19

Nose: Complex with violets and a hint of marzipan.

Palate: Savoury and subtle with damsons, rhubarb and black cherries, soft tannins and a fruity finish.

Comments: A lovely, medium-bodied red; the flavours will develop as the wine breathes.

STANLAKE PARK WINE ESTATE

Contact Details:
Waltham Road, Twyford,
Berkshire, RG10 0BN
01189 340 176

What3Words:
///imagined.reduction.putter

Website & Socials:
www.stanlakepark.com
@stanlakepark
info@stanlakepark.com

Visitor Centre: Yes, comprises a gift shop and wine bar. Open every day, excluding Mondays, from 9am-6pm (8pm Thurs-Sat). Wines are sold by the glass or bottle along with tasting flights and food. The £15 work-from-the-winery package provides Wi-Fi, hot drinks and lunch until 2pm, Tues-Fri.

Tours: Yes, throughout the summer: 11am Saturday and Sunday, 2pm Friday-Sunday, and 4:30pm Friday and Saturday. In winter, tours are at 11am and 2pm only. Tours last up to two hours and include a tasting of six wines – one at each stage of the tour.

Established: 1979

First Vintage of Current Owners: 2012

Size: 4 hectares

Grapes Grown: Reichensteiner, Schonburger, Pinot Noir, Pinot Meunier, Chardonnay, Seyval Blanc, Madeleine Angevine, Siegerrebe, Triomphe d'Alsace, Bacchus, Gewurztztraminer, Optima, Dornfelder, Solaris

Annual Production:
c 35,000 bottles, plus contract bottling

About 15 minutes' drive south of Henley-on-Thames lies the historic Stanlake Park Wine Estate, established in 1166 and known as 'Stanlake Park' since around 1500. Many of the current buildings, including the winery itself, date back to the 17th century. Numerous monarchs from Henry VIII to Queen Victoria have reputedly visited, including Charles II, who supposedly visited before meeting his long-time mistress, Nell Gwynne, nearby.

Ex-pilot Jon Leighton, whose family had owned the estate since 1952, first planted 500 vines in 1979 having recently returned from living in Australia. The estate changed hands in 2005 when the Dart family invested heavily in winemaking equipment, then it was sold again to the current owners in 2012. Some of the original vines still produce fruit, including what may be the first planting of Gewurztztraminer in the UK. The number of varieties is almost certainly greater than any other UK site.

STANLAKE PARK WINE ESTATE

The day-to-day running of the business is managed by Natalia Pezzone and Nico Centonze who joined in 2019. They met at university in Italy, got together in Argentina, and have since lived and worked in France, Romania and Italy. Nico is from a wine-making family based in Puglia and he's a viticulturist by training. Nico and Natalia see a formal understanding of farming as crucial, and Nico meticulously tends the vines as well as making the wines. Nico aims to make wines with balance, subtlety and good length. Natalia originally trained as a vet and then retrained at various vineyards, passing her WSET diploma with distinction along the way. She contrasts an artisan approach and Stanlake's listed buildings with her old Italian winery, which used to produce over four million bottles per year. Since joining, Natalia has launched the shop and wine bar, redesigned the labels, and changed the model from a predominately wholesale business to a hospitality business. Around 85% of the estate's production is now sold directly to customers. Stanlake remains an important contract winemaker for other vineyards in Oxfordshire, Berkshire and the Thames Valley, with contract winemaking amounting to nearly twice the volume of the estate's production. Around 30% of the estate's production is sparkling wine.

There are four vineyards within the 53-hectare estate. Reading University, one of Stanlake's biggest customers, visits every year and analyses the soil. There is huge variation from one row to the next, as well as between the different sites, with mainly loam, clay and chalk soils. The presence of water at the foot of the Ruscombe vineyard helps to keep frost at bay, although 40% of the crop was unfortunately lost to frost in 2020. Several trellising systems have been employed, but Nico was unhappy with some of the previous pruning methods and has changed them to optimise fruit quality and yield. Nico and two helpers do all the pruning to ensure every vine is perfect and the canopy allows for enough air circulation. Shropshire sheep keep the grass trim and fertilise the vines, beehives are kept for a local honey producer, and an abundance of wildlife – foxes, badgers and pheasants – visit the site. The grape-loving jackdaws, however, are less-welcome guests and are scared away shortly before harvest.

The stainless steel fermenters in the listed, 17th-century barn were installed during the 1980s by John Worontschak, now of Denbies and Litmus Wines. In a bumper year, such as 2023, the winery is at capacity. Different yeasts are used for different wines, depending on the desired style. The Barrel Room holds around 15 oak casks, mostly old, which impart subtle flavour and softness to the wines aged in them, including all red wines. Riddling and disgorging are also carried out on-site and are featured in the tour. Natalia aims to make the tours interactive and good fun, with a different wine tasted at each stage of the tour.

Around 100 weddings take place every year in a bespoke barn next to one of the vineyards, allowing the wine bar and shop to remain open and welcome patrons six days a week. Natalia, in her words, "always finds a second life" for anything that might previously have gone to waste. Used corks and bottles are upcycled into candle holders and decorations or are used by local schools. The shop also sells Nico's Italian wines, made from his family's Puglian vines.

Luxury accommodation in self-contained lodges on the estate can be booked online. Twyford railway station – easily accessible from London and Reading – is conveniently within walking distance. Stockists of Stanlake's wines include Echoes bar – run by Reading's Phantom Brewing Co. – in Henley-on-Thames. Wholesaler FCP Wines ensures the wines can also be found further afield. All Stanlake's wines are vegan.

Heritage Brut

Vintage: Non-vintage   **ABV:** 12%

Grapes: Pinot Noir, Seyval Blanc

Typical Retail Price: £25

Nose: Delicate pear and apple.

Palate: Light with a fine mousse and a long green apple finish.

Comments: Made by the traditional method and aged on the lees for 12 months.

Rosé Superior

Vintage: Non-vintage   **ABV:** 12%

Grapes: Pinot Noir

Typical Retail Price: £29

Nose: Strawberry and red fruit.

Palate: Red fruits with a smooth mouthfeel and long, creamy finish.

Comments: Made by the traditional method; very pale pink. The creaminess comes from two years' ageing.

Bacchus

Vintage: 2021   **ABV:** 11.5%

Grapes: Bacchus

Typical Retail Price: £16

Nose: Floral and more subtle than many Bacchus wines.

Palate: Grapefruit and citrus and not overly aromatic; integrated with a long, dry finish.

Comments: Bacchus wines are released a year after the other white wines which helps integrate and soften the flavours.

Orange

Vintage: 2022   **ABV:** 11%

Grapes: Siegerrebe

Typical Retail Price: £18

Nose: Melon and spice.

Palate: Complex, spicy and floral with good acidity and length.

Comments: Pale in colour for an orange wine; the Siegerrebe grapes ripen quickly, making them ideal for a contact wine. The pressed juice spends a week in contact with the skins and is fermented in oak barrels, resulting in a "concentrated white". Not oxidised in style.

Pinot Noir Rosé

Vintage: 2022   **ABV:** 11%

Grapes: Pinot Noir

Typical Retail Price: £16

Nose: Light bubblegum and pear.

Palate: Delicate floral notes and a long dry finish.

Comments: A refreshing and enjoyably dry rosé; a multi-award winner and Stanlake's best-selling wine. A short maceration results in the wine's pale colour.

The Reserve

Vintage: Non-vintage   **ABV:** 11%

Grapes: Dornfelder

Typical Retail Price: £16

Nose: Bright red fruit, similar to a Gamay.

Palate: Light and juicy with red fruits, soft tannins and good acidity.

Comments: The 2023 bottling is a blend of wines from 2020, 2021 and 2022, and some oak ageing adds smoothness.

WYFOLD VINEYARD

Contact Details:
Wyfold Lane,
Reading,
Berkshire, RG4 9HUT
07768 652 636

What3Words:
///deeds.replying.science

Website & Socials:
www.wyfoldvineyard.com
sales@wyfoldvineyard.com

Visitor Centre: Not applicable

Tours: Not applicable

Established: 2003

First Vintage Released: 2006

Size: 2.2 hectares

Grapes Grown:
Chardonnay, Pinot Noir, Pinot Meunier

Annual Production:
c 15,000 bottles

The Laithwaites have been in the wine business for over 50 years and have made wine in Bordeaux since the 1980s. Barbara Laithwaite has a passion for farming and, in the early 2000s, found Wyfold to be the perfect spot for producing English sparkling wines. Initially established with a friend and business partner, the site lies just a few miles from her family home in the Chilterns near Henley.

The first hectare was planted in 2003, with 4,500 vines of the three classic Champagne varieties: Chardonnay, Pinot Noir, and Pinot Meunier. The second hectare was planted in 2014, making a total of 9,500 vines. Half of the vines are Chardonnay, with Pinot Noir making up two-thirds of the remainder and Pinot Meunier one-third.

WYFOLD VINEYARD

The south-facing slope, situated down a winding single-track lane, receives maximum sunshine. A gentle westerly breeze helps keep frost at bay as the vineyard, 120m in altitude at the top of the slope, is high for an English vineyard and chilly at night. Pinot Meunier is planted at the bottom of the slope as its late bud-break makes it less susceptible to frost damage. The chalky, gravel soil provides good drainage and encourages the vines to lay deep roots in search of nutrients. The number of stones in the vineyard is striking and affects the farming of the plot; when the vines were first planted, the holes created to plant them had to be made manually using a hand auger.

Unusually, Barbara is a tenant at Wyfold, and she explains how the prospect of expiring leases affects some of her decision-making. With 2-3% of vines needing to be replaced every year, she is understandably keen to maximise their productive life where possible. This led to the creation of the 'Wyfold chop', where some vines reaching the end of their life are pruned back to the base to extend their productive life and produce new, healthy canes.

John Buchan, viticultural agronomist, provided advice on the vineyard set-up, as did English wine pioneer Mike Roberts, who co-founded Ridgeview in Sussex. Barbara manages the vineyard with help at key times, such as pruning, from local expert Ed Mitcham, in addition to family and friends. All varieties are trained using a double Guyot system. Barbara likes to be hands-on, highlighting how critical pruning is to the next two seasons' growth. She notes how farming practices have improved over the years, such as no longer turning and aerating the soil, which is better for the vines, better for worms, and better for preventing the release of CO_2. Sheep graze amidst the vines in the winter and keep the weeds at bay while fertilising at the same time.

Barbara particularly enjoys spring and early summer in the vineyard as everything is still "under control" and you can smell the blossom. Harvest time, which she describes as a "big relief", is another favourite. A local volunteer group, called Friends of Wyfold, helps with the harvest. Acidity and sugar levels are carefully monitored in the month beforehand to ensure the fruit is picked at the optimum time. One year, Barbara held her nerve and delayed the harvest until November 2nd.

Chardonnay is always picked last: one to two weeks later than the red varieties. Barbara is very fond of Chardonnay because it doesn't cause problems, unlike the unpredictable Meunier which she describes as a "wild child that doesn't do what you want". With a glint in her eye, she likens the three grape varieties to her own three sons, although she refuses to reveal which is which.

Wyfold's wines used to be made at Ridgeview, with the first rosé being made in 2014. In 2016, the first grapes were sent, rather more conveniently, to son Henry's Harrow & Hope winery just down the road in Marlow. There are no buildings or facilities at Wyfold: only a field in a rural landscape and a small shed with a kettle.

Wyfold's wines can, of course, be bought from Laithwaites. They are also stocked at several nearby pubs: the famous Crooked Billet, one of the first gastro pubs in Britain; the Highwayman Inn in Checkendon; and the Red Lion at Rotherfield Peppard. Retail outlets include The Henley Larder.

Wyfold Brut

Vintage: 2017   **ABV:** 12%

Grapes: Chardonnay, Pinot Noir, Pinot Meunier

Typical Retail Price: £39

Nose: Rich with pastry and yeast notes.

Palate: Citrus, minerality, a creamy mousse, and a good structure with plenty of acidity.

Comments: A blend of 50% Chardonnay, 40% Pinot Noir and 10% Pinot Meunier. A minimum of three to four years on the lees helps to give the wine structure and complexity. A very low level of sugar in the dosage keeps the wine bone-dry and close to extra brut.

Wyfold Brut Rosé

Vintage: 2018   **ABV:** 12%

Grapes: Chardonnay, Pinot Noir, Pinot Meunier

Typical Retail Price: £39

Nose: Bright red cherries.

Palate: A layered and long palate with red fruit, good balance and a lovely hint of sweetness on the finish.

Comments: A blend of 40% Chardonnay, 40% Pinot Noir and 20% Pinot Meunier. Small amounts of reserve wines from previous vintages are used to create additional complexity.

VINEYARDS
TO WATCH

Making a completely comprehensive guidebook is a difficult task, especially when the subject matter is as dynamic and fast-moving as the English wine industry. There are several vineyards I wanted to feature in this guide but, for various reasons, was unable. You can continue your exploration of local vineyards with the following:

FAWLEY VINEYARD
Fawley, Oxfordshire, RG9 6JA
www.gbvg.uk/vineyard/fawley-vineyard
Close to Henley-on-Thames, this is a very small-scale, one-hectare vineyard run by a family, more or less as a hobby. However, unlike many similar operations, Fawley's wines are commercially available, albeit difficult to find. The vineyard produces still and sparkling Bacchus, and the best way to get hold of them is from their small on-site shop, open on specific days in the run-up to Christmas.

HUNDRED HILLS
The Old Road, Stonor Valley, Oxfordshire, RG9 6HS
www.hundredhills.wine
@hundredhillswine
Close to JoJo's Vineyard and Pishill in the Chiltern Hills, Hundred Hills produces a range of upmarket sparkling wines at their modern winery. Gastronomic tasting experiences, including a tour, are available to purchase on their website. Their high-end wine can be found in over 20 Michelin-starred restaurants, as well as at Grape Minds, Henley Larder, and Eynsham Cellars.

SUNNYHILL VINEYARD
51 Cuddesdon Road, Horspath, OX33 1JD
www.sunnyhillvineyard.co.uk
@sunnyhill_vineyard
The closest vineyard to Oxford, Sunnyhill is a small, family-run business. Located just east of the city, it makes its own wines and offers tours and tastings in the summer as well as private events and alpaca experiences.

KINGWOOD
Kingwood Estate Ltd, Heathfield, Henley-on-Thames, RG9 4NR
www.kingwoodestate.com
@kingwoodestate
Situated on an estate, Kingwood is close to both Henley-on-Thames and Wyfold Vineyard in the Chilterns. Sparkling wine is produced and can be purchased via their website. Their 2018 Classic Cuvée won a silver award in the 2023 Decanter World Wine Awards.

THE GLOSSARY
& DIRECTORY

GLOSSARY

APPELLATION
The legally defined geographical area and rules specifying how a wine is made and where it is from.

BOUQUET
The aromas or 'nose' of a wine.

CELLAR DOOR
The area where wine is sold directly to customers – this could be anything from a small office to a large visitor centre and shop.

CONTACT WINE
A wine made from juice that has had a period of contact, after pressing, with the grape skins.

CORKED
A wine contaminated by the cork and hence with an unpleasant, musty aroma. The contamination is from a fungus called trichloroanisole (or TCA).

CUVÉE
A specific blend or batch of wine.

DECANTING
Pouring wine into a decanter or jug to expose it to air (allowing flavours to develop) and separate the wine from its sediment.

DISGORGING
The freezing and removal of the lees (sediment) from a bottle of sparkling wine. In French, 'dégorgement'.

DOSAGE
A small top-up of wine and sugar added to a sparkling wine after disgorgement. The amount of sugar determines the classification into Brut, Extra Brut, etc.

FININGS
Substances added to wine to clarify it by removing fine particles. Some finings are animal derivatives, for example egg whites, and prevent wines from being vegan.

GUYOT
A vine training system named after Frenchman Dr Jules Guyot. It usually entails the pruning of the vine's fruiting arms each year and then the training of either one cane (single Guyot) or two canes (double Guyot) along the lowest horizontal training wire.

LEES
The sediment, mainly dead yeast cells, left in wine after fermentation. Ageing wine on the lees ('sur lie' in French) can add body and creaminess to a wine.

MACERATION
The process of keeping pressed grape juice in contact with the crushed grape skins to impart colour, flavour and tannins.

MALOLACTIC FERMENTATION
The conversion of malic acid in a wine into lactic acid. Technically, it is not a fermentation but a bacterial process which produces diacetyl, often taking place in barrels. The process makes wines taste less sharp and imparts smoother, creamier or more buttery characteristics.

NATURAL WINE
General term referring to wines produced with no, or very few, additives, including finings and sulphites. These wines are often hazy and contain yeast.

ORANGE WINE
Wine made from white grapes but including a period of maceration with the skins and seeds (much as red wine is made) which creates a darker orange colour.

RIDDLING
The process of repeatedly rotating sparkling wine bottles, upside down, to gradually move the sediment to the neck of the bottle, readying it for disgorging.

SOMMELIER
A wine steward, usually with a formal qualification and/or a high level of wine knowledge.

SULPHITES
Sulphur dioxide, a preservative added to wines to prevent oxidation.

TANNINS
The bitter, astringent compounds in wine which come from the grape skins, pips and stalks. Tannins can taste like stewed tea in the mouth; they provide structure to red wines and soften over time.

TERROIR
The combination of climate, soil and landscape that influences the characteristics of a particular vineyard and the grapes it produces.

VINIFY
To make grapes into wine through a series of processes.

VINTAGE
The year of a specific grape harvest. A vintage wine is made wholly (or nearly wholly) from grapes of the specified year.

VITICULTURIST
Someone who studies and manages the science of vines and grape-growing.

WEIGHT
In wine tasting, the sensation in the mouth caused by the presence of alcohol; the concentration or intensity of flavour can also provide a sensation of weight.

DIRECTORY

VINEYARDS AND WINERIES

BRIDEWELL GARDENS

The Walled Garden, Wilcote, North Leigh,
Oxfordshire, OX7 3DT
Tel: 01993 259 059
Email: info@bridewellgardens.org
Website: www.bridewellgardens.org
Instagram: @bridewellgardens
Facebook: /bridewellgardens
What3Words: ///scarves.rivers.initiated
A mental health recovery charity, Bridewell provides support through therapeutic horticulture. Its gardens and organic vineyard are tended to by service users as part of their recovery.

BRIGHTWELL VINEYARD

Rush Court, Shillingford Road,
Wallingford, OX10 8LJ
Tel: 01491 832 354
Email: info@brightwellvineyard.co.uk
Website: www.brightwellvineyard.co.uk
Instagram: @brightwell.vineyard
Facebook: /brightwellvineyard
What3Words: ///radiated.sweetened.goal
Situated south of the River Thames, Brightwell's focus is on producing high quality still wines – particularly reds - though their repertoire also includes sparkling wines and an English brandy.

CHILTERN VALLEY WINERY

Old Luxters Vineyard, Hambleden,
Henley-on-Thames, Oxfordshire, RG9 6JW
Tel: 01491 638 330
Email: enquiries@chilternvalley.co.uk
Website: www.chilternvalley.co.uk
Instagram: @chilternvalleywinerybrewery
Facebook: /chilternvalley
What3Words: ///steam.afternoon.putts
Located in an area of outstanding natural beauty, Chiltern Valley is a long-established vineyard which boasts award-winning wines and a reputation for quality.

DAWS HILL VINEYARD

Town End Road, Radnage,
Buckinghamshire, HP14 4DY
Tel: 07833 462 597
Email: info@dawshillvineyard.co.uk
Website: www.dawshillvineyard.co.uk
Instagram: @dawshillvineyard
Facebook: /dawshillsparklingwine
What3Words: ///booth.sharpens.crystals
A hands-on and family-run vineyard that follows the wine from grape to bottle, producing both their wines and sparkling cider on-site. Daws Hill's wines are made using the traditional method and around 95% are sold directly from the site or at local markets.

FAIRMILE VINEYARD

Fairmile, Henley-on-Thames,
Oxfordshire, RG9 2LA
Tel: 01491 598 588
Email: cheers@fairmilevineyard.co.uk
Website: www.fairmilevineyard.co.uk
Instagram: @fairmilevineyard
Facebook: /fairmilevineyard
What3Words: ///poems.gates.impeached
*A family affair with a passion for producing excellent
quality sparkling wines. Fairmile's grapes – all classic
Champagne varieties – are used exclusively for their
own award-winning wines.*

FREEDOM OF THE PRESS

Ringwood Farm, Minster Lovell,
Oxfordshire, OX29 0ND
Tel: 07881 955 215
Email: gavin@freedomofthepress.co.uk
Website: www.freedomofthepress.co.uk
Instagram: @freedomofthepresswinery
Facebook: /freedomofthepresswinery
What3Words: ///basket.samplers.settle
*A small winery, urban in its ethos, that selects the
very best grapes for its wines. Crafted with minimal
intervention using high-tech equipment, Freedom
of the Press's wines are a product of passion,
expertise, and careful alchemy.*

HARROW & HOPE

Marlow Winery, Pump Lane North,
Marlow, SL7 3RD
Tel: 01628 481 091
Email: enquiries@harlowandhope.com
Website: www.harrowandhope.com
Instagram: @harrowhope
Facebook: /harrowandhope
What3Words: ///spend.swim.volunteered
*Run by Henry and Kaye of the renowned Laithwaite
wine family, Harrow & Hope is organically farmed
and focused on quality rather than yield. Though
rooted in years of tradition, they display a great
passion for discovery and experimentation.*

HENDRED VINEYARD

Allin's Lane, East Hendred, Wantage,
Oxfordshire, OX12 8HR
Tel: 01235 834 770
Email: info@hendredvineyard.co.uk
Website: www.hendredvineyard.co.uk
Instagram: @hendred_vineyard
Facebook: /hendredvineyard
What3Words: ///explained.bottled.optimists
*With south-facing, sunny slopes, Hendred has been
well-established in the Oxfordshire wine scene for
over 50 years. Concentrating on four grape varieties,
their award-winning still and sparkling wines are a
result of a long-standing dedication to their craft.*

JOJO'S VINEYARD

Russells Water, Henley on Thames,
Oxfordshire, RG9 6EU
Tel: 07967 637 985
Email: hello@jojosvineyard.co.uk
Website: www.jojosvineyard.co.uk
Instagram: @jojos_vineyard
Facebook: N/A
What3Words: ///spare.wonderfully.configure
Combining a passion for sustainability and traditional winemaking, JoJo's Vineyard – named for the owners' free-spirited dog – is a relative newcomer to Oxfordshire's wine scene. Though advocates for the unique benefits of technical innovation, JoJo's traditional method sparkling wines are produced with minimal intervention.

KIDMORE ORGANIC VINEYARD

Chalkhouse Green Road, Kidmore End,
Oxfordshire, RG4 9AR
Tel: 07818 011 690
Email: stephen@kidmorevineyard.com
Website: www.kidmorevineyard.com
Instagram: @kidmore_vineyard
Facebook: N/A
What3Words: ///loopholes.chopper.reservoir
Set against the backdrop of historic Kidmore House, Kidmore Organic Vineyard is another fresh face in the industry. Planted in 2018 and born from a passion for French wines, Kidmore focuses its efforts on producing top quality sparkling wines, with its initial line-up from the 2022 and 2023 harvests still in the process of being perfected.

LITTLE OAK VINEYARD

Paxford Road, Chipping Campden,
Gloucestershire, GL55 6LA
Tel: 07812 339 556
Email: admin@littleoakvineyard.com
Website: www.littleoakvineyard.com
Instagram: @littleoakvineyard
Facebook: /littleoakvines
What3Words: ///likewise.potential.fidgeted
Recognised in both nationwide and global award categories, Little Oak is, at its core, a family business. Passionate about providing a quality product, their harvest is always put to its best use, whether that's in their renowned sparkling wines or their Cotswold Gold Brandy.

OAKEN GROVE VINEYARD

Benhams Lane, Fawley,
Henley-on-Thames, RG9 6JG
Tel: 07792 633 987
Email: info@oakengrovevineyard.co.uk
Website: www.oakengrovevineyard.co.uk
Instagram: @oakengrovevineyard
Facebook: /oakengrovevineyard
What3Words: ///uptake.lakes.tastings
Nestled near ancient woodland, Oaken Grove is a picturesque vineyard which houses both an events space and an attractive wine terrace. The owner, Phil Rossi, is a true nature lover and is environmentally mindful in every step of production of his exceptional still wines.

POULTON HILL ESTATE

Poulton, Cirencester, GL7 5JA
Tel: 01285 850 257
Email: info@poultonhillestate.co.uk
Website: www.poultonhillestate.co.uk
Instagram: @poultonhillestate
Facebook: /poultonhillestate
What3Words: ///kilowatt.dozen.press
Situated on the edge of the idyllic Cotswold countryside, Poulton Hill is led by a small but passionate team. It prides itself on its proactive approach to welcoming visitors year-round via its tours and cellar door.

STANLAKE PARK WINE ESTATE

Waltham Road, Twyford, Berkshire, RG10 0BN
Tel: 01189 340 176
Email: info@stanlakepark.com
Website: www.stanlakepark.com
Instagram: @stanlakepark
Facebook: /stanlakepark
What3Words: ///imagined.reduction.putter
A heritage estate and one of the oldest wine producers in England, Stanlake Park has four vineyards of its own as well as a long history of being a contract winemaker for vineyards across Oxfordshire, Berkshire, and the Thames Valley. Alongside its tours, Stanlake boasts a gift shop and wine bar with indoor and outdoor seating.

WYFOLD VINEYARD

Wyfold Lane, Reading, Berkshire, RG4 9HU
Tel: 07768 652 636
Email: sales@wyfoldvineyard.com
Website: www.wyfoldvineyard.co.uk
Instagram: @wyfoldvineyard
Facebook: N/A
What3Words: ///deeds.replying.science
Exclusive, elegant, and praised by private chefs and wine critics alike, Wyfold produces award-winning English sparkling wines with a focus on quality, not quantity.

STOCKISTS, BARS, AND RESTAURANTS

BURFORD GARDEN COMPANY
Shilton Road, Burford, OX18 4PA
Website: www.burford.co.uk

CAFE DE LA POST
Cornerstone, Horseshoe Lane, Chadlington,
Oxfordshire, OX7 3BL
Website: www.cafedelapost.com

THE CHARLBURY DELI AND CAFÉ
Old Bank House, Market St, Charlbury, Chipping
Norton, OX7 3PL
Website: www.charlburydeli.cafe

THE COOKHOUSE DELI
14 Market Place, Wallingford, OX10 0AD
Website: www.thecookhousedeli.co.uk

DUKES WINE BAR
19 Duke Street, Princes Risborough, HP27 0AT
Website: www.dukeswinebar.co.uk

EYNSHAM CELLAR
43 Mill Street, Eynsham, Witney, Oxfordshire,
OX29 4JX
Website: www.eynshamcellars.com

FILLET & BONE
High Street, Chipping Campden, GL55 6AT
Website: www.filletandbone.co.uk

GRAPE MINDS
35 South Parade, Oxford, OX2 7JN
10 St Martin's St, Wallingford, OX10 0AL
Website: www.grapemindsdrinkalike.co.uk

THE HENLEY LARDER
3 Duke Street, Henley-on-Thames, RG9 1UR
Website: www.thehenleylarder.co.uk

JOLLY NICE FARMSHOP
Frampton Mansell, Stroud, GL6 8HZ
Website: www.jollynicefarmshop.com

MILLETS FARM SHOP
Kingston Road, Frilford, Oxfordshire, OX13 5HB
Website: www.milletsfarmcentre.com/millets-
farm-shop

THE OXFORD WINE COMPANY
6 Turl Street, Oxford, OX1 3DQ
165 Botley Road, Oxford, OX2 0PB
7 Little Clarendon Street, Oxford, OX1 2HP
Website: www.oxfordwine.co.uk

PAVILION DELI
25 Market Place, Henley-on-Thames,
Oxfordshire, RG9 2AA
Website: www.pavilionfoods.co.uk

Q GARDENS FARM SHOP
Milton Hill, Steventon, Abingdon,
Oxfordshire, OX13 6AB
Website: www.qgardensfarmshop.co.uk

TEARDROP BAR
Unit 22, The Covered Market, Market Street,
Oxford, OX1 3DZ
Website: www.teardropbar.co.uk

MISCELLANEOUS

THE THAMES VALLEY AND CHILTERN VINEYARDS ASSOCIATION (T&CVA)

Website: www.thameschilternsvineyards.co.uk

HENLEY CYCLES

16/18 Duke Street,
Henley-on-Thames, RG9 1UP
Website: www.henley-cycles.co.uk